ADVANCE PRAISE FOR *WHAT REMAINS*

"Do we ever stop learning to live?

"Channeling Zen and the *Art of Motorcycle Maintenance* and a healthy dose of Kerouac, Otterbacher embarks on a great American journey of self-examination and discovery. Searingly self-aware, driven by curiosity, John takes seriously Rilke's injunction: 'Let everything happen to you.' He holds nothing back, racing ahead where others fear to tread, on a trip that is pastoral one moment and harrowing the next. We're along for a glorious ride in this spare and daring travelogue of the heart."

Hank Meijer, author of *Arthur Vandenberg*

"John Otterbacher's *What Remains* beautifully blends a late-life adventure across an often overlooked America with brutally honest self-evaluation. His erudite tangle with age, declining abilities and increasing vulnerabilities, while maintaining a vibrant desire to live fully, is both entertaining and an essential guide to everyone. In his eclectic view as a psychologist, survivor, former legislator, family man, and adventurer, Otterbacher delivers humor, dramatic scenery and provocative insights into both his inward and outer journey down a road rarely travelled."

Steve Callahan, author of bestselling *Adrift*

"John Otterbacher invites the reader along for an unforgettable, transformative journey through time, space, memory, and into the future. The sense of openness and curiosity with which he encounters everything – from the most sublime to the most painful – offers the reader a model of attention and awareness. This memoir changes the reader. After reading *What Remains* the world and its inhabitants appear more familiar and also more extraordinary. The place to which this remarkable journey returns us is more meaningful than it was before, and, having seen through the eyes of this great writer, we more easily see and appreciate what we might otherwise overlook. "

Laura Kasischke, author of *Mind of Winter*

"John has a way of befriending the stranger in the coffee shop, the dog outside and the reader of this memoir. He laughs at his foibles and makes it easier for us to laugh at our own. This old man on a motorcycle has a mystic's eye for our connection to each other and all of life. *What Remains* is a great ride, one I encourage you to take."

Barry Johnson, author of *And,* Founder of *Polarity Management*

In this book,
the author blends sections and events
from two cross-country rides into a single narrative.

WHAT REMAINS

MEMOIR OF AN OLD MAN ON THE ROAD

JOHN OTTERBACHER

First Edition, 2021

Copyright 2021 by John Otterbacher

For information about permission to reproduce selections from this book or bulk purchase for educational, business or sales promotion, contact barbara@barbaracraftlaw.com.

Library of Congress Cataloging-in-Publication Data has been applied for.

What Remains/John Otterbacher

Contents: Memoir – Aging - Travel – Motorcycles – Survival - Coronary disease -Mindfulness

ISBN 978-1-7376995-1-4

Printed in the United State of America

Credits:

Cover design by Willem Mineur

Interior Design by Angela Morse

Production Assistance: Pierre Camy

Cover photo by John Otterbacher

Eerdmans Publishing for vignettes incorporated

Further information can be acquired at:

www.johnotterbacher.com

To Barbara, John Ryan, Kate and Erin,

Darcy, Annabelle and Nate,

both wind and harbor

"Old men ought to be explorers
Here or there does not matter
We must be still and still moving
Into another intensity."

TS Eliot

"All writing is autobiography...
all autobiography is storytelling."

J.M. Coetze

PROLOGUE

The wail of a siren in the distance, lurching to a stop on the road beside me. An intense young man in dayglo yellow bounds out of the vehicle and kneels down. He peppers me with diagnostic questions. Yes and no will do. He flexes a pair of industrial scissors, then curses under his breath when he can't cut through the canvas skin of my motorcycle jacket. He changes to a pair of metal cutters. He carves his way up my right sleeve and pries the jacket open. Shattered carbon plates spill out on the sand between us.

He rocks back on his heels and wipes the sweat from his eyes. He scissors away my t-shirt and begins to examine me. He feels my swelling arm and shoulder, then down along my ribcage. He does not seem pleased.

"There's a lot of blood pooling in here, and I'm afraid a lot of breakage." He shakes his head and grimaces. "We'll get an IV going. And we're going to need a helicopter."

"Helicopter?"

He looks at me evenly, then the scar down the center of my chest.

"Heart?"

"Yup."

"How long ago?"

"Twenty years."

He nods and leans in, speaking softly.

"I don't want to be disrespectful, Mister, but you're really busted up. We have to get you to a trauma hospital. And we don't have a lot of time."

RIDE

"Everything you've ever wanted
is on the other side of fear"

RALPH WALDO EMERSON

"We taste and feel and see the truth.
We do not reason our way to it."

W.B. YEATS

CHAPTER 1

BURNING DOWN, a stillness. The spent urgency of people saying goodbye. I hold Barbara afterwards, her head on my chest, unwilling to let go. She tussles the hair on my stomach.

"Have fun tomorrow, John."

"I love you too."

Her breathing slows and softens. She slips into the deep sleep I want for myself. I do not follow her, adjusting and readjusting, trying not to wake her. I am desperate for the renewed energy morning will demand. I cannot fall asleep.

Is this fear or excitement? Probably a little of both.

I am good at fear, something I learned back in the neighborhood. In those days size was everything, in my case a lack of it. Being a runt did not play well in our working-class confines, on the playground early, the basketball court or football field later. Most of all on the

streets or down the back alleys where my younger
brother had an uncanny knack for starting fights I felt
obliged to finish. Finish was often a two-fisted whaling I
would pronounce a victory if my tormentor, tired of
pounding me, threw up his hands and walked away. By
the time a growth spurt leveled the playing field at
sixteen, an underdog mindset was in place, both grit and
hesitation.

My only opponent these days is a mulish resistance
to aging, the face in the mirror when I ease out of bed
and into the bathroom.

"Not looking so good, Johnny boy," a lame attempt
to make light of weariness.

I am too exhausted to answer, also wide awake. I
open the medicine cabinet and reach for the Tums. My
stomach is acidy with anticipation.

I close the medicine cabinet and glance back in the
mirror.

"Sure you're up to it, Bozo?"

The last couple of years have taken a toll. I have a vague
but growing sense of vulnerability in spite of daily exercise and a long walk most evenings. Back spasms can
sideline me for days on end if I overdo log stacking or
most anything else. The blood thinners that ease the
ache in my heart turn shaving cuts into exercises in
patience and compression, and elevate the danger of

bleeding out if the chainsaw gets away from me. Hesitation is creeping back into my life, invading my lifelong and admittedly adolescent "can do" outlook. It's hard to deny, especially tonight, a few hours before hitting the road.

I click off the light, straggle back into the bedroom and stand by the bed watching Barbara sleep. I do not want to wake her with my thrashing around. She has to leave early for a breakfast meeting.

I move past her into the study and inhale the books I love. My desktop is never this empty. Ever. I walk over to the windows and look out at Lake Michigan, an almost eerie silver under the September moon.

Our dog, Finnegan, wakes up and pads in to join me, shaking the sleep out of his head so violently he almost topples over. He looks up, forgives me with a slow swish of his tail. We wander through the rest of the house together, pausing to take in every room. I try not to think I am saying goodbye.

CHAPTER 2

I GO BACK to the bedroom at first light, lift the sheet and slip in next to Barbara. She does not wake, but reaches over to touch my leg. I follow her into sleep.

She is gone when I wake up. She's made coffee and taken Finnegan to doggy daycare.

She has left a note in front of the coffeemaker on the counter.

I love you.
Please be safe.
I'm not done with you yet.

I splash cream in my coffee and sit down at the table that looks out at the lake. It is dinnertime again, a month ago.

"Been thinking," to Barbara over lasagna.

"Really?" A playful smile.

"It's been a while since I unplugged."

"I'll say."

"Even longer since I've been out riding."

"Sure has," and when I say nothing, "What do you have in mind?"

She's smiling broadly now, absolution in advance. "I know you have something in mind."

I'm not ready to leave yet. I get a yogurt out of the refrigerator, a handful of pecans for good measure.

Cold feet, Johnny?

I pour another cup of coffee and sit down at the table, more comfortable with memory than climbing on the bike. A few more moments of *then* before taking on *now*.

The nights have gone cool as the clock runs down. We take out blankets we put away in June. The sun is sinking into the lake earlier each day. Evening's light gets more dramatic as summer humidity gives way.

I talk with Kate one weekend, Erin later on the phone. Taking a cue from Barbara, they give their hesitant blessings. Erin closes our conversation with a distinctly mixed message.

"If you die out there, I will kill you," a special kind of tough love, I guess.

I hold off discussing my plans with John Ryan until he's settled into his fall teaching schedule. He would like to join me but knows the difference between thirty-nine with a family and fancy-free seventy-four.

"Age does have its advantages, Dad."

At a weekly get together, I tell friends I will be away for a while.

"Three, four weeks, a motorcycle ride. Get reacquainted with backroad America."

Several glasses stop short of open mouths.

"Three, four weeks, alone, on your motorcycle?"

"Yup," more sheepishly than I intend.

"Where you headed?" more question than challenge this time.

"South, then west. There's a lot of beauty between here and California."

Nobody says anything for a moment, which says everything.

Finally a bald-faced "What are you thinking?"

I take a long swig, how to explain.

"I could use some time out in the wide open, what's left without all the commotion I call normal. What matters and doesn't at seventy-four. What I've learned, what I'd like to change. How to make the most of this old man stretch. That kind of thing."

A few nods. They're trying.

"But why the motorcycle? It's dangerous."

"Yeah, it is, if you don't pay attention. Hell, it's suicidal if you don't pay attention. But that's also the point. I spend way too much time up in my head, over-thinking. The cycle doesn't put up with that. It demands focus. The road with its imperfections and surprises, what's coming at you right now. Pay attention or die."

Nobody says anything.

"As weird as it sounds, I calm down when I ride. And wake up. Both. Simple as that."

Too many words.

"Besides, it's fun."

It's moving up on ten o'clock. Time to get on my way if I'm going.

I clean up the kitchen and pull on a boot, lace it up and pull on the other.

Then I freeze.

All the questions I've been swatting away turn back on me, less questions than bare-knuckled fears.

You are seventy-four years old, John. Are you sure you want to do this? Three thousand miles of back roads on a twenty-year-old motorcycle?

What happens if that bike breaks down in the middle of the nowhere? Or you do?

Your back or your heart, out in desert west Texas?

I stand up and walk out onto the deck, the relief of motion. I don't want to pretend. I've got some fears and a few hard-to-answer questions. Can I just be okay with that?

I'm down the steps now and walking, wishing Finnegan were with me, out along the ridgeline to a point high above White Lake. It's as calm today as Lake Michigan was last night, everything I am not. My long-deceased mother walks alongside — "When are you going to settle down, Johnny?" — shaking her head with sham exasperation, then breaking into a grin.

My father joins us, his sad, smiling grace as Parkinson's takes his car keys, then his life.

"Do it while you can," he whispers. "You can rest later."

The big step is between zero and one, the distance from *maybe* to *yes*.

I pull on my yellow dayglo jacket and adjust the internal crash panels over my elbows, shoulders and back. I reach into the pocket of my jeans and finger the tiny bottle of nitroglycerin I keep there. I walk out to my motorcycle, check the oil and tires, then step back.

I love my bike.

A 1995 Honda that I bought for nothing, she's carrying a lot of miles — just like her owner. In the short time we've been together we have become good friends. She's a better motorcycle than I am a driver, a natural athlete's agility and power. She will get me through.

"Let's do this."

I cinch down the travel bag that rides behind me, put on my helmet and pull the chin strap tight. I slip my riding gloves into a side pocket. I want to feel these early miles.

I swing my leg over the seat and sit down. It feels good. I click the engine switch and hit the starter. The engine engages and settles into a comfortable purr. I squeeze the clutch handle and shift into first gear. I let out the clutch and we are off.

As much as I love words, I don't experience life in complete sentences, especially on my Honda. Images and impressions mostly, that I try to make sense of later.

These first miles are slow and hesitant, arms spastic, too cautious in the curves. *Less control*, I remind myself. *More attention.* To the tire-rupturing pothole I might see too late, launching me God knows where. To the oncoming driver looking down to text and sliding over the centerline. And especially on these tree-lined back roads, the driver looking for a car rather than a motor-cycle and pulling out of a driveway in front of me. The road wants all of me. There's no room out here for front page headlines, the agitation they invite. Miss the gravel in the curve ahead and I'll be kissing pavement.

There's a lot to attend to for a mind that wanders, the autumn rust gathering in the trees, the old woman in her front yard, bread crusts flying, the flourish of wings. It's why I'm out here, the raw experience pulsing beneath my frenetic thinking.

I am beginning to relax an hour out, no passing cars for miles.

I slow when I come up on a truck piled high with hay. I realize too late that a bale on top is working free, tumbling onto the road and exploding. I swerve hard through a storm of hay, power by, then drift back into my lane. I am wide awake and trembling, a familiar stirring in my chest.

The road intersects with the interstate an hour later, a gas station and a McDonald's. I pull into the McDonald's, park and dismount. I take off my helmet and stretch long enough for my back to uncoil. I shake the stiffness out of my legs.

My first steps are those of a creaky old man, insistent about a restroom. The afterschool crowd quiets when I step up to the counter. I order a diet coke and take it outside to stand in the sun.

I am joined by a member of the McDonald's brigade, traces of ice cream down the front of her uniform. She looks me over, my Honda out beyond, and lights up a cigarette.

"Nice bike."

"Thank you."

"My daddy had one, something like that."

When I say nothing, "Hard to sell it when he went and got old."

"Happens."

"Two uncles rode them too."

"A family motorcycle gang."

"Yeah, but it didn't work out so well."

"How's that?"

"They both died on 'em."

Tongue tied, I say nothing.

"One of 'em drove right under a flatbed trailer."

I've got nothing.

"The other — you might not believe this — collided with his best friend's truck on the way home from work."

"Damn."

"Damn right. His friend never did get over it."

"I'm sorry." Lame, but the best I've got.

We stand silently while she takes two deep drags.

"Well you be careful out there, Hon," and flicks her cigarette butt out into the parking lot.

"Gotta get back to work."

I walk back to my bike and pull the helmet over my well-roiled brain. I yank hard on the chin strap, as if toughness will erase the dour history she shared. I start the engine, look both ways, and throttle onto the service road and up the freeway entrance ramp, flicking the blinker and swiveling around for a visual, then accelerating hard into a seam in the rush-hour traffic. An easy seventy-five settles me into the flow.

There are a lot of us in this traffic clot, too many shifting parts. I follow a truck as he eases out to pass the slower one ahead. I'm into a blast of heat and fumes now, eye level with tires I pass, then power into the lane that opens up, an empty road ahead.

I'm not fond of expressways, but they are efficient, safer also in their numbing sameness, taking the curve out of every curve. No driveway surprises, no mailbox grannies, no freewheeling family pets.

But I'm not wedded to time or destination. It's the *getting* not *arriving* that matters to me, the necessary presence a two-laner serves up to an overheated brain.

I cross the line into Indiana and stop at a welcome center, stuffing a free map under the bungee behind me to look over later. I get off the expressway at the next exit and take a sleepy road into the countryside.

The forested hill country gives way to flatland, farm after farm, past abandoned houses, angular and empty, rusting equipment and collapsing barns, overgrown two-tracks and corporate spreads carpeted with the stalked remains of harvest. I pass an occasional pickup, summer blond grasslands, the roadside parks my parents favored, a straggle of signs announcing a town.

I slow as I enter, grain elevators, groceries and gasoline, past kids pulling a dog in a wagon, a barbershop, tractor supplies, pizza place and bar, a garage with the hood up on the truck out front, and way too many "for lease" signs. I slow further to pass a school and a football field with a single aluminum stand. Then a string of one-story bungalows, yards mowed close and American flags, grandma waving from a porch.

I power through hay and alfalfa country, strobed light in the trees from the plunging sun, into shadow-land now, green going khaki, haze gathering at the edge of fields, deer in the fading light, high beam on the asphalt, hunger building, the unity of night.

I see a city glow out ahead, relief with the arrival of suburban houses. A good run and done.

I pass a gas station and a fast-food joint, signs for an expressway ahead. I have second thoughts about a restroom stop and swing into a party store parking lot to turn around. I pull up to a steep exit, look back for traffic, and brake as headlights come up from behind. My boot slides on loose gravel when I step down to balance the bike. We pitch to the left and over, an engine rev, my helmet hard against the asphalt. I kill the engine, curse, and crawl out from under the bike.

A guy in a van pulls up behind me and jumps out, lights on, motor running.

"You okay?" he shouts and runs up to me.

"Yeah, I am," pushing my visor up and shaking my arm. "But not my bike."

The left mirror housing and turn signal are dangling from a wire. Gas is bleeding from under the bike.

"Could you help me lift it up?"

The gas stops running when we muscle the bike upright. We back it up onto the flat surface and ease it down on the kickstand.

"I am okay now," and thank him. He goes on his way.

When I reach up to release the chin strap on my helmet, blood is dripping off the fingers of my left hand. I pull a handkerchief from my hip pocket and press hard into the seam on the top of my hand.

"Can we help you?" Two police officers run up, tossing cigarettes behind them. "State Police," gesturing to the police post behind them.

"You guys are fast," I grimace. "My bike is banged up a bit, but I think we're okay."

They look down at my hand, the circle of blood leaking through my handkerchief.

"That doesn't look okay. Let's call a medical rig to check you out."

"I'd rather not, Officer. It's just a surface scratch. I'm on blood thinners. I bleed like a pig, but it'll stop with pressure."

He's looking at me, incredulous.

"I'm okay. Really."

It takes a while to get the police settled down and explain how I dropped my bike. I thank them for checking in on me. They finally head back across the parking lot.

"You come over here if that bleeding doesn't stop."

I work the damaged turn signal back in place and try to breathe away the heaviness in my chest. It doesn't work. I pop a nitro under my tongue and walk slowly to the end of the parking lot, trying to let go of the self-recrimination I'm so good at.

I slip out of my jacket to avoid getting it bloody, and drape it over the handlebar. I lift the handkerchief and look. The blood begins to seep again, doesn't want to stop. I press the handkerchief back down and walk over to the party store. I glance around when I enter, see no one, and move quickly to the restroom. I lock the door behind me.

I pick some of the gravel out of the cut and turn the faucet up high to finish the job. I replace the handkerchief with paper towels and press hard. I check my elbow in the mirror, the beginning of a bruise.

I lift the paper towels to check my hand, still bleeding down the fine line of the cut. I pull down fresh paper towels.

I am in the restroom for a long time, something not lost on the counter clerk when I emerge. She gives me a good looking over, the scuffed jeans, the helmet wedged under my arm. Her eyes narrow when they go to the towels I am pressing against the back of my hand.

"Sorry to bother you," nodding at my hand, "but I took a spill out there and I have an owie."

Her annoyance gives way to a suppressed smile.

"Boys!" and a stage-worthy sigh. She wags her head, lips pressed tight. "I've got two of them at home."

"I'm wondering if you have some band-aids or tape, something to stop the bleeding."

"I'm sorry," what looks like concern, "went looking for band-aids a couple days ago. We've got nothing."

"Duct tape? Anything?" Almost sheepish now.

"Geez, I am sorry. Don't have that either."

It's a small cut, but a bleeder. I've got to close it enough to climb back on my bike.

"How about scotch tape?"

"We do have some of that I think." She rifles through a drawer under the counter.

"Ah," satisfaction flooding her face.

I drive down the expressway to an exit announcing cheap motels. I stop at an open drug store for gauze pads, tape, and antiseptic cream. I check into a bargain motel within a block of an IHOP, lock my bike and take my gear to the room. Rather than turn on the TV as I too often do, I flop down on one of the beds and stare at the ceiling, numb with exhaustion. I feel like an old man.

I am an old man, a notion I playfully scoff at when I'm around my aging friends. "Make no concessions," I exhort them, speaking most of all to myself. Truth is, I am almost shocked at my age, what Tolstoy called "the biggest surprise". Old and worn, denial more difficult with this aching hand.

There is no denying my rumbling stomach.

No dinner for me if I don't get going. I pry myself off the bed and out of my protective jacket, its weight more obvious than this morning. I flick on the bathroom light and spill my patch-up supplies onto the counter. I pull the scotch tape off — damn, that hurts — and bleed into the hot water blast from the nozzle. I lather on disinfectant which stops the bleeding, cover the cut with a gauze pad and tape it down tight. I give my face a washcloth workover and hurry out in search of some-thing to eat.

The over-buttered pancakes deliver, the coffee I should not be drinking this late.

I swallow hard when the waitress asks "Is there anything else, Sweetie?" in that saccharine tone too often reserved for white hairs.

"No thank you, Miss," no edge in my voice. "Hit the

spot," which probably cements any old guy notions she might have.

"What time do you close?"

"Not soon enough," she tells me. "Eleven."

"I'd like a decaf then."

I pull out my iPhone and scroll through emails, nothing that demands a response. Then I flick to the news summaries, overriding my resolve to abstain.

The waitress saunters back with a refill. I thank her and take a sip.

"Any room for dessert?"

I'm an easy mark this hour of the night.

"What do you have that's chocolate?"

She describes an ice cream and brownie concoction, stopping mid-sentence for a swipe of the tongue. "And lathered with dark chocolate, whipped cream and a cherry."

"Sounds like a winner."

I take out the note cards I carry in my hip pocket and jot down some impressions from the day. "Fell down" gets its own card, one I'm not likely to forget.

Just a pen in my hand takes me back home, the ease with which I let the world push into writing time. The bedlam I call normal starts with the clutter I accumulate on my desk. Add to that the ping of incoming emails, the unscheduled phone call of a distraught client, as if the daily "things to do" list is not enough. Even more challenging is the way my thoughts ricochet off my scribbling, every word calling up an alternative, every idea. In the late afternoon the tyranny of time kicks in, the unyielding mix of expectation and imagination. How about this? Or this? The avalanche of possibilities, crazy-making if I let it, competing for the moment, this pen on this page.

This.

It is not surprising I like the focus motorcycling demands. For a brain addled with ideas, focus feels like relief.

It's not the only reason I'm out here, not by a long shot. But I do want a vacation from electronic devices, the unrelenting intrusion of factoids and happenings. I am making one phone call a day to Barbara, and maintaining phone availability to the kids. I will check my emails once a day, largely for emergencies.

A single day of abstention clears out some mind space.

I need all the mind space I can get.

The waitress returns with a mountainous dessert. I take a bite and return the spoon to the plate.

I have gulped so much of my life. This is a season for smaller bites.

At my age, I don't find *should* and *shouldn't* that helpful. I prefer to do my own reckoning, and learn from the consequences of decisions I make. Any *should or shouldn't* worth its salt just ends up making sense.

I do have a few bosses these days, most notably a prostate that leads me around like a little boy. He wakes me before dawn and tells me it's time to get up and go. I roll out of bed, no questions asked, and stumble into the bathroom.

I peek between the blinds before climbing back into bed. It's still dark outside. I sag back onto the mattress, trying not to fixate on how age has eroded my capacity to sleep. Too often I toss fitfully until sheer exhaustion takes over. This is one of those nights. I lie awake, shift around to find comfort, and lie awake some more. Early evening's clarity gives way to doubt and second-guessing.

What happened out there tonight? How did I let it happen?

I tell friends that I'll get old later. Is that just empty bravado?

Have I lost more than I am willing to admit?

I fall back to sleep before dawn, uncomforted by answers.

CHAPTER 3

I WAKE IN BRIGHT DAYLIGHT, wash, and pull my gear together. I give the cycle a thorough going over, special attention to turn signals and brakes.

I am underway before ten.

I pull in at an Einstein's Bagels a few miles down the road and park cautiously, chastened by last night's drama. I order a large coffee and an egg and cheese bagel, sitting inside for a few minutes, then moving to a table in the sun out front. The sun feels so good that I buy another bagel.

A wizened old black man watches me over his newspaper several tables away. He gets up in time, warm smile and nod, and ambles over to the table next to mine.

"Nice bike, young man."

"That's very kind of you, but I'm not so young. Thank you anyway."

He studies the Honda for a minute, the travel bag behind my seat.

"Mind if I ask you where you're going?"

"Not at all. I'm headed south for a while, then west. Maybe California."

"A fur piece."

"Lots of little pieces, really. Stop when I want, rest when I need to."

"Sounds like you've got it all planned out."

"Not really. Just following the most interesting back roads I come across."

"I'd probably get lost."

"Me, too. I'll check the map every night, circle the last town I went through."

He says nothing for a while, then starts chuckling.

"Gotta hand it to you, Mister," eyes bright and a grin. "You're a rangy one."

I stop at Purdue on the way out of town and make my way to the university bookstore. I'm always interested in what the kids are getting pushed at them in their writing and literature classes. I try not to buy anything, as there is limited room on my bike. I take a brisk walk around the campus afterwards, soaking up the sheer vitality of the place. My Fitbit tells me I've walked two miles, miles on which my blood-starved heart relies.

I think of how writers Marcel Proust and James

Joyce met just once, at a party in Paris during the twenties. They were joined in what could have been a remarkable conversation by the composer Stravinsky and painter Pablo Picasso.

In Harold Bloom's telling, the conversation cycled down into the health woes of aging, Joyce with his headaches, Proust with his florid indigestion. Stravinsky and Picasso tired of the conversation and stepped away, chose to focus instead on the beauty around them.

Age is real, ache and decline, the stiffness I feel when I climb back on my cycle. But so is beauty, the energy it calls up.

I get back on a two-laner and head south, a series of long curves through the woods. Then it's out into farmland, hay fields crowding the asphalt. I pass through an unsigned intersection, three stark white crosses on the corner.

I downshift behind a massive Dollar General truck. I follow it for what seems like forever, yellow centerlines on one side and corn fields on the other. I finally get by him in a crossroads town, past potbelly grain elevators and their silo-shaped elders. There's a swarm of wind generators out on the horizon, slow and silent in the breezeless heat.

The sun turns against me by midday. I motor on as if in some fevered hallucination, a long stretch of dips and lifts, like sailing the swells off Casablanca thirty years ago. Up and over and down again, crest and trough off a rocky coast. I make a westerly tear an hour later, bike shuddering in the backdraft of semis I pass. Hawks circle on rodent patrol over cornfield flats, then trees and hills near the state line.

Lightheaded now and thoroughly parched, I exit at an Illinois welcome center, the faint smell of something burning.

———

I spend the better part of an hour in thrall of the air conditioning inside, alternating between restroom, drinking fountain and maps on the wall. I am no fan of the map-driven efficiency too often imposed on travel. I prefer to think of a map as a menu of options. The USA map gives me a lot to work with, including distraction from concerns about the Honda.

I looked it over thoroughly before coming inside, and could find nothing to explain the lingering scent. I go back out to check the tires for signs of wear and find none. I pop the panels off the engine compartment and look for trouble. Nothing. I want to think I've just pushed too hard, that she simply wants time to cool off.

I am all too aware of my mechanical incompetence, a source of both uncertainty and entertainment before Barbara, John, baby Kate and I first took to sea. When friends expressed concern about our going, Barbara would lighten the conversation with sham incredulity.

"You should go to sea with an engineer. I'm going to sea with a poet."

But that's another story.

It's uncertainty I take back out to the cycle. I suit up, climb on and twist the ignition key. The engine turns over once, then nothing. Again, and nothing. How can the battery be dead? It has been charging all morning. I yank off my helmet, frustrated with my incompetence.

Dead is dead, and I've got to get it going, if only to drive somewhere to get answers. While I'm pacing around helplessly, a young black man pulls his semi into a truck lane across from me. He leaps out of the cab and sprints to the restroom. I consider going over to close his door but think better of it. He smiles good-naturedly when he emerges minutes later.

"Damn, that was close."

"I know the feeling."

He walks over to his truck and slams the cab door, then arches his back and looks over at my bike.

"Old Honda, isn't it?"

"Ninety-five."

"Road trip?"

"Was, until twenty minutes ago."

"Twenty minutes ago?"

"Been riding all morning, but the battery's dead. Not charging for some reason."

Most people would back away at this point. He doesn't.

"We could push start it."

"You'd be willing to help?"

"Sure. Been there myself. I'll sure enough be there again."

"I'd appreciate it."

I'm already pulling on my helmet and zipping up my jacket.

"Get on it," he says. "I'll do the pushing."

I do and he does, shouting just as the engine catches.

"What goes around..."

Out of nowhere there's an honest-to-God Honda dealership sign, left at the next exit. Amazing.

The engine sputters on the exit ramp, then dies altogether at the stoplight on top. A bright yellow Camaro pulls up behind me as I climb off and start to push. He shouts something and blows by, horn overriding the Beach Boys. I stop long enough to drape my dayglo jacket over the back of the bike, then wave traffic around me as I push.

There was a time when pushing the Honda would have been easy. Not now. A series of heart attacks and less-than-successful surgical interventions in the late

1990s banished my running shoes to the closet forever. In a desperate attempt to restore my health, Barbara and I committed financial suicide by returning to the ocean, this time with our two youngest kids. Our six, healing, bare-budget years at sea saved my life. None of it would have been possible without a shared sense of adventure and twice daily handfuls of medication.

This is the heart I am working with, twenty years later. So I push for a while, stop to breathe, then push some more. I slip a nitro under my tongue when I need to, get back to pushing when the pressure lets up.

I'm soaking wet by the time I spot the Honda sign down the road.

Thank God for Warren. From his graying flattop to the oil black boots, he's a motorcycle marine: calm, logical, no-nonsense. Everything I am not at this point, everything I need to be.

He starts with a crisp "how can I help you" and will not take his foot off the pedal until the job is done. He and his tattooed team remove the fairings and work their way through the wiring. They come up with a diagnosis in less than an hour.

"Your regulator's burned out," and he shows me.

"You're lucky it didn't catch fire."

He retreats to his office and returns minutes later.

"I can get a new one from Canada, if you want. There will be an overnight charge."

"Best option?"

"Only option, if you want to get back on the road tomorrow."

"Let's do it."

Warren's counter clerk takes me out back when I ask about the possibility of sleeping on their property.

"I could roll out a sleeping bag and save a buck."

She seems entertained — *crazy old man* — and laughs, hand up over her mouth.

"You'd have to wait until we leave for the night, and be outta here before seven in the morning. And," leaning in and whispering, "I'm not telling you any of this."

I look around after she walks back into the show-room. It seems like a good idea until I come across the picked-over bones of what looks like a large cat, twenty feet from where I intended to roll out my sleeping bag.

I shower and cool off at the motel down the street. I slide a book into my hip pocket and head in the direction of the University of Illinois campus, hoping to find the bookstore before it closes. I'd like to get into those writing and journalism stacks, put my hands on some cutting edge instruction manual they force on their graduate students. I am energized by how little I know, how much I have to learn.

The store is closed by the time I get there. I sit down on a bench outside to cool off and send a text to the kids. I fiddle with the iPhone I purchased before leaving, a complicated upgrade from the flip-phone I've relied on for years. "Had a lot of good wear left in it," my father would have said. Unfortunately, it didn't. I puzzle over its shiny replacement, can't figure out how to send a text.

I'll call Barbara later. She can smoke signal assurance to the kids.

I can't think of our kids without smiling. I like who they are, how they're making their way. John Ryan is teaching at Tribeca-Flashpoint film school in Chicago and running his small production company on the side. His wife, Darcy, is teaching inner-city kids with a doggedness I cannot fathom. Their daughter, Annabelle, is sweet, smart and full of herself. One of us.

Young Kate, the family engineer, spends her days trying to break futuristic vehicles at the GM proving grounds before they take them to production. Her boyfriend, Nate, is doing much the same thing with future-model trucks. They spend many of their weekends rebuilding *Grace*, the family sailboat they are purchasing from Barbara and me.

Our youngest, Erin, fresh out of nurse residency at Mayo Clinic, will finish her doctorate next year. Her longtime boyfriend, Khaleb, also teaches inner-city kids in Chicago.

I can trust them to fashion my inability to text into a chapter in their handbook of good-natured derision.

I spend the early evening walking the business district near campus. Not a single bookstore is open. I'm trying not to dwell on the Honda or my inability to fix her.

I am who I am, no more or less.

Besides, if the nature of adventure is not knowing how it turns out, isn't incompetence part of the adventure?

I haven't eaten anything since breakfast and am getting hungry. I pass a string of bars and restaurants, stopping at ones that look interesting. I check out menus, noise levels and lighting, hoping to read while I eat. I am getting too finicky and it's getting late.

A sign tells me to wait for the hostess inside the restaurant I finally choose. She arrives in a flurry, a less than invitational "how can I help you?" in spite of the singsong lilt of her voice.

"I'd like a table for dinner, under a light bright enough that I can read."

She inspects the vacant space around me.

"Are you alone?"

"Yes I am."

She leads me to a booth in the back.

"Will this be okay?" She's trying to be kind.

"Perfect."

I take the book out of my pocket and slide in. She puts the menu down in front of me.

"Your waitress will be right over."

"Thank you."

While studying the menu, I register the twinge of disappointment I felt at her less-than-enthusiastic greeting. It shouldn't matter, but it does.

My heart is talking to me on the walk back to the motel, an uncomfortable heaviness in my chest.

It is a perfect time to stop for an ice cream cone — "double chocolate, please" — and a few minutes to let my heart settle down.

I sit down on a bench in front of the place.

The ice cream and ache take me back to my father. We are watching TV in my parents' living room. His heart is shot, but it is not what will kill him. The Parkinson's he has lived with for fifteen years is closing in around him, taking him over. His world is literally bursting into flames, larger and larger doses of medication distorting his perceptions.

His hand flutters up from rest in his lap, gesturing at an eruption of fire on the rug in front of the TV.

"Do you see that?" turning to me in alarm.

"It's the meds, Dad. The meds."

I know about fire by now. I have seen my own life burst into flames. First a heart attack, mild but unexpected. Three months later, another. After surgery, another. Not my father's imprisonment in withering neurology, tremors that will only get worse.

Fire none-the-less.

"It's ok, Dad," reaching across to take his hand and smile reassurance.

"Supper's on," Barbara calls from the kitchen where she and the kids are helping my mother.

I get out of the chair and stand in front of my dad. He takes my extended hands reluctantly, then hangs on tight, a proud man embarrassed by his inability to get out of a chair unaided.

I step aside when he gets to his feet. He staggers a bit, then reaches some tenuous equilibrium. I walk just behind him as he shuffles around his chair, through the dining room and into the kitchen.

We breathe a collective sigh of relief when he plops safely into his seat at the table. An unsteady voyage to be sure, but no head-banging dive in the direction of the Frigidaire.

I sit down at the table across from him, a place I have relished since childhood. Eating with my father is a primetime event. He doesn't just like food, he adores it. I'm not sure he would win an eating contest with our dog Finnegan, but it would be neck and neck at the finish line.

Dad lights up when the platters arrive. His lips move eagerly as his plate is filled, silverware in hand. Then he's all in, first forkful making its tremulous way mouthward, food falling off as it goes, shaking aggravated by annoyance, scraps tumbling down into his lap. He throws what is left on the fork into his mouth, then glares down into his lap with disgust. The muscles tighten in his jaw. He exhales indignation. He looks up at me, mouth set, and shakes his head in frustration. *I get it, Dad.* Then the beginning of a grin — *How does he do that?* — a smirk and a nod, all smile now, eyes flooding with warmth.

We collapse into our chairs in the living room after dinner and listen in silence to the clatter of dishes from the kitchen. We look at each other and smile our good fortune. This is what we have – plenty – in a small room filling up with flames.

And this is what I have now, a melting cone and a still soft night. The slow erosion of age on my frail ego, lunacy when vanity wants more. The unintentional but real condescension. Small losses, simmering, unlike the flames my father dealt with.

Can I learn to live with his grace?

CHAPTER 4

I TAKE my time in the morning, lingering over breakfast and a free newspaper.

Warren calls before noon.

"The bike should be ready in fifteen."

I pack in a hurry and go to the front desk to settle up.

The woman behind the counter recoils from my helmet like it was a loaded gun. She squints worry at me when she hands me a receipt.

"Be careful out there."

"Will do," I assure her, then turn back when I get to the door.

"Thank you for your concern."

I lug my gear down the street toward the garage, over lawns that run to the curb. Three or four yards down I cross a cemetery named for Lincoln, try hard not to step on the graves. I also try not to think about crashing.

My bike is standing outside the display room, her cherry-red finish ignited by the sun. I go inside, pay Warren and thank him, then head through the doors marked "Employees Only."

It must be break time. Two of the mechanics are sitting at a picnic table near the open garage door. Another is pacing back and forth out beyond them, pulling hard on a cigarette and exhaling like a yogi.

"I want to thank you guys," shaking greasy hands, "for getting me back on the road."

The one outside tosses his cigarette and high-fives me when I approach.

"Get out there where you belong."

Another shouts from behind as I head for the door.

"You're living our dream, old man."

———

I soon tire of the two-lane road south of Urbana, pinched in by the corn pushing up to the road.

I cut over to the nearby expressway the first chance I get. It's not much different, only corn at a distance, corn and more corn as I bang out the miles.

I merge with the snowbird migration heading south, license plates from Wisconsin, Minnesota and Michigan. An occasional boxy motor home joins us, slowing the arterial flow to the sun.

I swing into rest areas to stand behind my white-haired brethren at urinals, waiting for something to happen. Fresh arrivals line up behind us, wringing their hands and pacing their urgency. They stumble into the parking lot afterwards, eager to get back on their way.

The traffic tails off in late afternoon, time to find a motel or campground for the night. I lean hard into the open road, too aware of the day I have lost. The wind tunnels through every vent in my jacket, robbing the heat of its weight. After an hour without being passed by anyone, I am finally overtaken by a sleek black Lexus that I follow until swinging off for an overdue stop.

I get ice water and a diet coke at a McDonald's. A pencil-thin woman walks up to a table across from me. I can hear her coming, tray in one hand, phone pressed to her ear with the other. She is speaking in Spanish, shouting really, then slams her tray down on the table and stomps outside. Her outrage is muted when separated by a window, full volume again when I walk by her on the way to my bike. I don't have to speak Spanish to know someone's in the doghouse.

I am trying to avoid freeways on this trip, their exits overloaded with mega chain restaurants with generic offerings. I'd rather prowl the back roads with their serpentine unpredictability and offbeat specials at mom and pop joints. But it's miles I'm after this afternoon, and the fastfood efficiency the interstate delivers.

The prairie gives way to low hills in southern Illinois, parched fields, midget corn and gullies full of underbrush. Brown yields to leafy green near the Ohio

River. The temperature drops and gives me a second wind.

I am not ready to roll out a sleeping bag yet.

I cross into Kentucky and get off the interstate, stopping at a gas station on the outskirts of a small town. It has a single pump outside, raising questions about the freshness of its gas. I walk inside and pay for "whatever six dollars buys me." Even if the gas is less than good, I can dilute it by filling up down the road. The clerk seems disappointed I am buying so little, and responds to my attempts at small talk with wordless nods and a lot of "Yup."

I get back on the road into western Kentucky, soft hills, curves, and tree-lined straights. Hawks circle above small farms, playing with the breeze while scouting the fields for a late-afternoon snack. An occasional driver comes up fast and roars by, impatient with my gawking. It doesn't bother me. Even with a late start I've piled up the miles and am riding for fun now, dips and rises, afternoon's heat gone lush and balmy. It could just as well be west Michigan. Fields and woodlots drift by, prosperous farms, beautiful after the numbing sameness of the interstate.

I cross into Tennessee at dusk. The terrain is similar to Kentucky's, but with harder edges. Shadows creep out over bone-colored fields, mist gathering under bushes at their border. Headlights swoop up from behind, flashing brights, then blasting by.

I wind my way into the bluffs and bottomland of hill country. Boarded up farmhouses squat in overgrown yards, eaves drooping, missing shingles, abandoned farm equipment and trucks. A half mile on I pass well-groomed houses, windows lit bright and manicured lawns, ponds and white fences and mailboxes that dazzle.

Night is closing in, and with it an uncomfortable sense that I'm out here too late. I throttle down a notch when passing clusters of trees along the road. An invitational glow is gathering on the underside of clouds ahead, the possibility of a town. It's none too soon as the deer are on the move. I glide by two does, then come up over a rise to find a buck standing in the center of the road. His head is up, horns high, but he is looking the other way. He turns toward me when I flash my brights, bounds off the asphalt as I ease down on my brakes, racing alongside me now, pinned in by a rockface next to the road. I brake hard when he bolts across in front of me, disappearing as I slide to a stop.

There had better be a town ahead.

I pull into the third budget hotel of the trip, a largely unlit "executive" something or other. Backroad budget, I remind myself, life in out-of-the-way places. I sit on my bike for several moments, too tired to drive further.

I get off, catch my heel on the travel bag and stagger out into the parking lot, steadying myself and straightening up in slow motion. I have a lot of tied-up parts. I arch my back and roll my shoulders, try to twist the stiffness out of my neck. I take the first unsteady steps in the direction of the motel office.

The young woman at the check-in desk has trouble taking her eyes off the textbook she is studying. Her dark eyes brighten when she does, a welcoming "how can I help you?" with a hint of Indian-English.

I negotiate my AARP discount and pay, take the room key without an inspection. I'm not eager to see what I've purchased, but I'll take whatever they've got. Anything more than a bed and a shower is a bonus.

The clerk leads me out and around a corner and points to a darkened door across the parking lot.

"There's good food at the Mexican place down the road, but you'd better hurry. I think they quit serving at nine."

It's eight forty-five and I'm way past hungry.

There are several cars in the parking lot out front, easing my concern about missing dinner. I almost knock over a "Seat yourself" sign when I stumble in, find an empty table and sit down. I don't have to wait long before a waitress shows up, light on her feet, menu in hand. She looks me over with a good natured "I don't know you!" to which I have no reply.

"Well..." I nod, feigning embarrassment. "You've got me there," which I want to take back immediately.

She forgives my awkwardness with a hand on my forearm and a warm "that's not very fair of me, is it?"

"Well..." a default grin, an "aw shucks" shake of the head.

She steps back, barely suppressing her laughter, and cocks her head.

"Let me try again," sham gravity now. "How can I help you, Mister?"

"How about that menu, a glass of water and a draft?"

"Yes, sir!" she quips flirtatiously, "Back in a minute," and heads toward the bar.

There are couples at every table, talking to each other or sitting painfully mute. Couples and a tired old guy waiting alone for his beer. I reach back to my hip pocket for the book I have forgotten to bring. I could go back to the cycle to fetch it, but decide it's better to sit here than hide behind a book.

A woman glances up from her dinner to study me. I feign nonchalance but I know better. It would be so much easier to be dining with Barbara or friends.

The waitress delivers a foamy beer, and with her pleasantries a reprieve. Too late. I am exposed, my simmering need to be thought well of. Part of why I'm out here, I remind myself, the clarity solitude provides. On this night the stark and obvious extent to which I rely on others to prop up my fragile sense of self.

I preach allegiance to Plato's "know yourself," to airy Socrates' "examined life." Nice words, but how do they play on the road alone?

What's left of me without my beloved books and lofty thinking, my ease with words and comfortable others? Without the action-hero mythology in which I have conspired? What remains when I am stripped bare, beneath the filmy surface of my life?

The waitress eventually delivers three greasy enchiladas, a pile of rice and some over-processed beans. Perfect. Not the larger answer I am looking for, but answer enough. Self-interrogation can wait. A first steaming forkful up under my nose, a smell, a taste, fork back on the plate between bites. Thirty minutes of enjoyment rather than the usual ten. Progress.

"Didn't like it a bit, did you?" Blue eyes is back.

"Spectacular."

She waves a dessert menu in front of me. I decline.

"More than enough," an admission I don't make often.

I sign at the bottom of a MasterCard imprint.

"Thank you for a wonderful meal. It's been fun trying to keep up with you."

"You, too, Cowboy."

I linger for a few minutes, a full stomach's answer to

exaggerated introspection. Still alone, I am more comfortable than before.

A young couple has ordered drinks at a nearby booth. She has dark hair and eyes, and is leaning in to watch him. He is thumbing his phone furiously, then pausing for a reply. He does not even glance at her. She folds her hands in her lap. The seconds tick away. He thumbs on, eyes riveted to his phone. She sits, says nothing. Only looks. Her feet begin to fidget under the table, minutes now, ankle over ankle and back again. He does not look up, not even a glance.

I get up to leave, stomach roiling.

There are many ways to be alone.

I have never had a healthy relationship with sleep. I apparently quizzed my exhausted mother regularly with "why go to sleep and miss life?" If she was to be believed, I'd occasionally run to the end of my rope, literally collapsing while sprinting across the backyard, being carried off to bed sound asleep.

Tired as I am, I am not ready to give up my evening walk. I check my Fitbit, then head up a gravel side road into a night so dark it dissolves any sense of place. I stop every now and then to roll my head around until the ache in my neck gives way. I walk for a while, then start over again.

Clearly I need to ease up a bit, get off the road early

enough to avoid playing tag with Bambi. If I get tangled up out in antlerland, I am likely to end up on the asphalt. I can just as well roll out my sleeping bag at dusk, get a sunrise start in the morning.

I can use some slowing down across the board. I regularly question our national hyperactivity as a society-sanctioned way to avoid life's deeper questions. The sorry truth is that I find it easier to pontificate about stillness than to be still. My unease in the restaurant tonight. My exaggerated concern about how others might perceive me. I tell myself I can learn from anything. What can I learn from that?

I stop again, arms above me, reaching and breathing and letting go. I have a lot to let go of.

The road dead ends. I turn around and start back to the motel. I listen to the fevered call of tree frogs in the darkness, music of a sentient world. A pumpkin moon eases out above a distant stand of trees.

Back at the motel, I sit down on a mattress encased in plastic. It creaks when I climb in and shift around to get comfortable. Annoyance gives way to amusement in time, still later to open laughter.

CHAPTER 5

I WAKE UP REFRESHED. I strike up a good-natured exchange with the man in the mirror while brushing my teeth and shaving.

"Could use some help with self-awareness, Plato.

"Where's Yeats with his 'mirror turns lamp'?"

Nothing but silence from either of them, in spite of their flaunted way with words.

Over coffee and oatmeal, I'm reminded of Buddha's dictum, something about being your own lamp.

I am looking hard for easy street.

The road south is as potholed as a Michigan freeway in spring. It chains me to the here and now. Nothing matters but the twenty yards ahead, weave and dodge on a broken road. There is no way I can do this all day.

I make the first stop much earlier than normal, climbing off to shake the cramps out of my hands. I have blisters on two fingers from gripping so tight.

I have pulled into a station out of the 1940s, pillared overhang above a single gas pump. Lots of cracked stucco. There is no credit card access outside, just a hand-scrawled sign that says "Come on in." There are ancient cover girl calendars on a peeling wall inside, the models' eyes averted as if to say *Look, but don't touch.* This is exactly what the old guy behind the counter is doing, oblivious to my entering. He chuckles without embarrassment when our eyes finally meet.

"Caught me," his rheumy eyes brightening.

"Yup," I smile back, but doubt that he hears me.

I fill my tank and pay him. I ask him how to get to a better road — shout really — and he shouts back directions. I thank him. When climbing back on my cycle, I remember a friend's elderly father admitting that he thought a lot about women as he tottered into senility.

I merge with a smooth four-laner in the early afternoon, relieved to have oncoming traffic a lane away. I roll through long stretches of pine. Not the white pine giants of nineteenth century Michigan, but not scrub pine either.

I pull off at a Mississippi welcome center to get a free map and a hot cup of coffee. Before leaving I ask an attendant about bookstores in the area, the rich literary South and all.

"I don't much do bookstores" she demurs, "lots of other stuff" and peters out.

I thank her and head for the parking lot.

I get off at the first sign to Oxford. I take a two-wheeled saunter through a parade of pine, lull and rhythm, drift and glide, long looping arcs through sun and shadow, pulse-quickening bends, swing and soar and engine thrum, into the tree-lined Oxford town center.

Oxford sheds her gentility on the afternoon before a home game. The town center is a traffic hive. I spend a sweaty half hour circling an open-air parking lot, finally inching into a shared space with a Harley growler. I lock my helmet to the handlebars and drape my jacket over them to dry.

I will drive a hundred miles in the rain to spend time in a good bookstore. There's no rain today in the home of legendary Square Books. I cross the courthouse square and walk in. Up above the high shelves are pictures of America's most acclaimed authors, pilgrims each to this spirit site of writers. I begin a slow perusal that will take me into the early evening.

The front tables are full, but not with best sellers. Here are the books I won't find at the big chain stores, the outliers and off-centered others. The ones I long to buy but don't have room for. I gather up an armful and go upstairs, surprisingly uncrowded on this pre-game afternoon. I spread the books on a table in the tiny café and rent the space with an iced coffee and scone. Over a period of hours I sample each book, winnow my options down to three or four favorites and begin again. At closing time I emerge with a softcover small enough to carry in my hip pocket.

I push into the low-grade pandemonium developing on the streets and walk all four sides of the town square. This is a big game weekend, more people than the place can comfortably handle. There is no place to turn without bumping into someone, a first whiff of claustrophobia.

It's not much better when I make my escape into a nearby restaurant and settle down at a table in what seems like a quiet corner. I order a burrito the size of a Volkswagen and get a foamy local draft. The place is filling up quickly now. Barbara phones two bites into the burrito, salsa down the front of me as I fumble for my phone. I am happy to hear her, phone clamped against one ear, hand over the other. I must be shouting because I get the stink eye from two young women who stare their disapproval.

"Can't talk now, Barb. I'll call back in a few minutes."

I leave my book and reading glasses beside the savaged burrito and move into the fray looking for a restroom. I am way out of place here. The bar is churning with coeds and their avaricious suitors. I work my way through a herd of alcohol-glazed fraternity boys, circling like sharks in a well-chummed sea.

I follow a gesture down a hall into the crowded confines of the men's room. There's an overflow line at the urinals, groaning revelers shifting from leg to leg as they wait. I slip by them to a stall, toilet bowl in the embrace of a puking partier. He's finished, I guess, stands up and flushes – "Sorry" – and moves by me. I stand over the toilet listening to the verbal jousting out in the corral. Someone shouts, "Take your time, Mikey," followed by a chorus of "Yah, Mikey." Someone else whines "I'm tired of sleeping alone" to a thunder of "yes" and "me too."

I head out through an unsteady procession of guys streaming the other way. I am surprised to find my burrito untouched when I get back to the table, my book, glasses and beer. I take a few mouthfuls and pay the waiter. A booth full of students give me forced smiles when I push by into the open bar area, past "where you from?" and "I'm done taking shit from him."

A group of young women muscle through the door in front of me, the ringleader shouting "time for some of that silent treatment" over her shoulder to her posse. It all seems like a lot of work to me, more evidence of age.

Friday night is on fire out in the street, crowd heat and holler and a whole lot of alcohol. Students mostly, letting it rip, and a few traumatized parents in town to check on their darlings. What was a party an hour ago has tilted in the direction of frenzy. Throngs of young men out on the prowl, gaping and awshucking when they lose their balance, "I'm so sorry" diluted when they burst into laughter further down the street. Police in dayglo are out in force, moving on horseback through the crowd, stopping to bellow at the worst offenders with handheld megaphones. Someone's in a load of trouble if they have to dismount.

It's a scene I am eager to escape. I head to the parking lot to check on my bike. A few people are milling around there, stragglers mostly, sharing a joint, too addled to handle the bedlam. The Honda is fine. My jacket is damp with the evening dew. I leave it draped over the handlebars and walk out beyond the party glow in search of a place to sleep. A motel is out of the question tonight, booked weeks in advance for tomorrow's big game.

I call Barbara as I wander through the surrounding neighborhood looking for a park. She's a little jumpy at the prospect of my sleeping in a park. I try to calm her before we hang up, then walk up and down the darkened streets long enough to finish off the day's four miles. I find nothing that resembles a park.

I am tired now, a staggering exhaustion at the end of a long day. In desperation I settle on a strip of lawn at the well shadowed end of a pricey hotel parking lot. I go back and retrieve my bike. I throttle hard when I return to the hotel entrance, coast in silence down the length of the parking lot. I pull into an empty spot beside a hulking dumpster.

I roll out my sleeping bag in the shadow behind the dumpster. I pull off my boots, slide them onto the grips of my handlebars, and lay my jacket over them. I push a tent pole into the ground and use it to drape mosquito netting over the mouth of the sleeping bag. I slip out of my jeans and into the sleeping bag, pulling the mosquito netting around me.

The sky is clear. Although I am only four blocks from the town square, the night is still. I am warm and tired and slow to sleep. I keep thinking of our daughters and their campus years, the desire to be noticed without being reduced to an object.

CHAPTER 6

I AM shocked awake by the hydraulic growl of a dump truck lifting the dumpster above me and stopping. I roll away from what feels like danger, and scramble out of my sleeping bag. I stagger to my feet and lock eyes with the driver. Each of us is surprised. He shakes his head as he might with a teenager, then re-engages the lift. He hoists the dumpster up over the top of the cab, a rush and clatter, garbage aroma and dust. Then he swings the empty dumpster back out over me, and jerks to a stop. He shakes his head again, trying to suppress a smile, then slams the dumpster to the ground in front of me. I jump out of the way. I cannot see him when he backs up and revs the engine, a cloud of diesel fume when he roars away.

I grab my jeans off the ground and lean against the dumpster to wrestle them on. I collapse the tent pole, gather the sleeping bag, pad out into the parking lot in my stocking feet. I check my watch. Four hours of sleep and this shock of morning.

I roll up the sleeping bag and pack everything away. I soak a washcloth with canteen water and scrub hard, face and neck, up under my armpits. Nothing is stirring in the parking lot. I brush my teeth, pull on clean socks and a t-shirt, and finger-comb my hair in the uncracked rearview mirror. I catch myself grinning.

I head off to what I hope will be breakfast in the town square. I find a coffee shop and walk inside, trying not to notice the eyes studying me above lifted newspapers. I sit down with a coffee and a newspaper someone has left behind.

It feels like a clean getaway.

―――

I stop at William Faulkner's "Rowan Oaks" estate on the way out of town, curious about anyone who writes. I spend an hour on a guided tour through his house, a while longer wandering out under the oaks. A great storyteller, he was as quirky as anyone in his books. When quizzed about what critics considered a narrow-margined lifetime in Oxford, he replied "I've got all the stories here that I could ever hope for." And he did, including his own. Legend has it that he slipped a black snake into the bedroom where his daughter Peggy's fiancé was sleeping.

"Just introducing him to a family friend" Faulkner

later explained. It's a story this snake phobic could have done without, and likely will not forget.

———

I drive further south into Mississippi, swinging west towards the river as the sun heads for the horizon. I stop hourly for water and get out of the sun. The asphalt is so hot in front of a small-town gas pump that I shift from one foot to the other to ease the burn radiating up through the soles of my boots. I catch a glimpse of a skinny old man watching me from inside. He is craning his neck to get a fix on something. He studies me intensely when I come in.

"Can't quite make out that plate, Sonny," squinting and flicking his tongue. "Where you from?"

"Michigan."

He blinks and says nothing.

"I'd like to get something to drink and use the restroom if you have one."

He points down an aisle, and shouts "coming through" to someone out of view. I shut the door behind me and pull up the toilet seat, which keeps falling back down. There's a well-worn copy of Penthouse sprawled open on top of the toilet box.

Someone passes the door bellowing "Michigan?" and, after a pause, "No thank you."

Whoa.

I wait a few moments – is he done? – before stepping out. He's standing at the counter a few steps ahead of me, broad shoulders and matted hair, a red t-shirt sweated through between the shoulder blades. He turns around to glare. He has scar tissue layered up on both of his cheeks.

"What you lookin at?" when our eyes meet.

"Nothing in particular."

"Nothing in particular, eh?" Nodding now, pursed lips collapsing into a weasely sneer.

I do not break eye contact. He says nothing. Just stares.

I've lost all thirst for water. I thank the old man behind the counter and step over to the door. I turn the handle —*slowly, John* — and pull, step out into the oven.

I walk out to my bike slowly, shoulders squared, and fasten down the tank bag. I stand beside my bike and tug on my gloves. *No rush, John.* I swing my leg over, settle in, and put the key in the ignition. He hasn't come out yet. I pull on my helmet and open the visor, pull the chin strap tight. Still inside. I swipe the kickstand up with my heel, hit the ignition, lean over the Honda – "Let's get out of here." I squeeze the clutch, shift and release, and am rolling now, slowing to look both ways, then swinging onto the road to the right. I hope I am heading west.

I drive for a while before checking the rearview mirror, as if I were not shaken.

I am shaken.

What happened back there?

He could have been bluffing, just messing with a Yankee. I certainly was bluffing, feigned nonchalance a thin veneer over fear.

I would feel better right now if I weren't riding alone.

Since that first ride to California in 1971, I've always ridden alone. The only exception I make is when riding with our son, John Ryan, or with Barbara to local haunts.

I like it that way. I leave when I'm ready, head where I like, and stay out for as long as I want. No Harley group discussions, no need for consensus, no one but myself to blame for bonehead decisions.

But this is different, the full heft of alone. The intensity of solitude I claim to want. Raw fear also, and nobody with whom to dissipate it.

I am sailing this ocean alone. Not for the first time, but alone nonetheless. On the high seas and flying, slowing for a pothole, greasy tar snakes through a languid curve, the unwelcome wiggle when a tire gives way, past fields of soybean and low-slung cotton, sagging farmhouses, dozing cattle and bullet-riddled road signs, a dead dog, bloated, and flattened black snake, "available" billboards with a number to call, out over the centerline, pay attention or there'll be hell to pay.

I am not ready to stop for the night.

A cloud of bugs splatter against my visor at dusk. They work their way up my sleeves and into my clothing. A sign appears in the headlight ahead, a tire shop, the beginning of a town. I stop at the first bargain motel I see, eager to get out of the heat. I remove my shirt, debug myself, put my shirt back on and enter. A smiling pudge of a woman welcomes me, hands me the sign-in sheet and a pen. My sweaty forearms stick to the countertop as I fill it out.

"You can use our washer and dryer if you need to."

"Thank you. I need to."

"I'm giving you a room on the first floor. It's cooler than the ones upstairs."

She assures me I can park in front of my room, a lack of competition in the empty parking lot.

The room is cool as promised. The shag carpet sticks to the soles of my boots on one side of the bed. It seems clean otherwise, asks forgiveness with a Bible for the cigarette burns on the shade of the bedside lamp.

I flop onto the sagging mattress and reach for the remote, delighted to find a football game on a TV too dated to inspire much confidence. I peel myself off the mattress to remove my boots and climb out of my clothes. The bed feels cool when I collapse back on it. I wake up in the fourth quarter of the game, too late for my nightly check-in with Barbara.

Some days it seems my memory caught a midnight train and is living in a suburb of Kansas City.

When I finally drag myself out of bed, I fish out my flowered swimming suit. There's no pool but there is that promised washing machine for my ripening road clothes. I give myself a once-over with a wet washcloth and re-arrange my hair with my fingers. I slip into the swimming suit and a fresh t-shirt, a clean pair of socks and the construction boots I ride in.

I step back from the mirror in a mock pose, "Nice look, Johnny." If only the kids could see me now. It is fun to embarrass them, small payment for what they put us through as teenagers.

I sag back down on the bed to tie my laces. I rub road dust off my legs, the shrinking calves and transparent skin. A thin white scar snakes from ankle to groin, fading souvenir of open-heart surgery. I've earned every bit of it, I tell myself. I'm fortunate to have what I have.

I feel a twinge in my back when stuffing my stand-alone jeans and their sweaty companions into the washing machine. Road wear or gas station tension? I want to think it's the honest ache from a demanding day on the road.

I plug a handful of quarters into the washing machine. It rattles itself into a frenzy as I cross the parking lot in search of dinner.

I find a ma and pa restaurant squatting in a gravel parking lot several blocks down the road. The screen door complains when I pull it open. I am greeted warmly by a middle aged African American woman when I enter. She hands me a menu, then steps back to look me over, special attention to the flowered turquoise swimsuit and construction boots.

"My, my, what do we have here?" she announces to everyone, smiling broadly. A group of elderly black men swivel around to join the festivities.

"Now you've got to admit that I'm looking good."

She cackles and looks back at her patrons.

"He got all dressed up for Saturday night!"

Laughter all around, and for the better part of dinner. Chicken dumplings to die for. Large helpings of good-natured back and forth, "Reallys" and "I'll says" when I admit my age. A few generous "no ways" and an oft-repeated "all the way from Michigan." "Can't say I ever," with nothing to follow. Several rounds of "motor-cycle you say," and "Hmm, hmm, hmm..." when conversation lags.

"I feel bad about rousting you fellows out," when the

manager returns with a broom. "But we all got church in the morning."

A lot of "yes, Ma'am," and "Better get on home" as they stagger to their feet and pause to straighten up.

I get up and shake hands with each of them as they file by, my "nice talking to you" and "thank you" far short of enough.

I am astounded by their warmth, men younger than me and far and hard older.

More evidence of the randomness of things, the uneven price of being human.

I wait a few minutes for our hostess to finish sweeping, then pay my bill, thank her, and walk outside. I stop long enough for my eyes to adjust before starting back to the motel. There's a fevered commotion in the scrub brush beyond the parking lot, a yelp and thrashing, a single blood curdling shriek. Then silence. I stand stock still, a surge of adrenalin and short little breaths. Distress gives way to a deep and immediate sadness, more sadness than the situation warrants.

I ride alone for the nourishment that silence provides, what's left when words get out of the way. This silence is unbearable, this sadness. I feel more alone at this moment than I can bear.

I put my clothes in the dryer when I get back to the motel. It refuses to provide any distracting clatter. I shower off the day when I return to my room. I climb into bed and pull the covers up around me in search of warmth. Exhausted, I want to fall asleep. I don't.

The night's small savagery behind the restaurant drags me back to childhood. I am down at Highland Park with a group of neighborhood kids. We are wrapping up a successful afternoon catching tadpoles and frogs from the flood waters that engulf a public golf course each spring.

The light is fading, time to head for home. I'm already late for dinner. We are crossing the last fairway to where a path leads up the ridge toward home. A commotion erupts over near the fifth green, a knot of boys swirling around and shouting. They are swinging sticks at a shadow on the ground, darting this way and that to escape their mayhem. My friends drop their containers and run toward the action with whatever poles and sticks they have. I do not follow, moving up the path, at some point stopping to look back. They are attacking a rat driven out of the sewer and into the open by the flood. Already injured, he is dragging his greasy hindquarters behind him, helpless against the hacking and stabbing and clubbing. They descend on him with ferocity and excitement. Nobody listens when I shout, "Stop!" I am a stranger in this world, an alien.

CHAPTER 7

IT IS sunny and warm by the time I retrieve my clothes from the dryer. I pull on clean underclothes and jeans, then check the state map for the nearest bridge across the Mississippi. It feels good to get underway, even without a morning cup of coffee.

I angle down through a series of small towns, trailers and churches and fried food joints. I pull into a station for coffee and gas. A group of old black men are sitting at a picnic table under a willow tree across from the pump. They are engrossed in a game of chess. When they shift in their seats or get up to stand, they do so wearily. A lifetime of labor, I suspect, too hard or too long from the look of it. I want to think the next generation has an easier go of it. I am not sure that is the case.

I walk inside and pour a cup of coffee, overload it with cream to offset the bitter taste. An ancient black woman sits smiling behind the counter, wrinkles and squinted warmth.

"Nice motorcycle."

"Thank you."

"Where you headed?"

"West. Not sure beyond that. Probably dip down into Texas."

She hums her approval.

"Well you have fun out there." No mention of safety or survival. Fun.

"I'll do my best." I take my coffee outside.

Does the later version of a person have to be a pared down version of the original? A paler version?

Why must the old man banish the young? Why not gather up the boy and take him along?

I drive out onto a bridge over the jaw dropping Mississippi. Awe is undermined, then obliterated by a hail of cotton balls off a flatbed truck ahead, an unbroken shower from the rolls he is hauling. Cotton puffs bounce off my visor, harmless but a distraction from staying in my lane. I pass him when we spill off the bridge into Arkansas, too late for a sustained view of the river.

The road bends to the northwest, with no obvious offshoots to the west. I pass luxury homes with docks out into a long lake to the right, rundown trailers and bungalows off to the left. Miles of this, the easy intoxication of a smooth road on a soft, warm day.

The sun is not where it should be. I study every intersection I pass for a road that will take me west. No luck. I pull off at a gas station to find out where I am.

The news is not good. The counter man grins and tells me that I have missed two turnoffs that would have taken me west. I feign nonchalance to take the wind out of his enjoyment. Truth is I am angry at myself. For all my incompetence, I don't often get lost.

I go out to my bike to get a map, then back in to splurge on a chilled bottle of coffee. I open the map on a table for the second time today. It feels like a concession. On a map that highlights the best roads in red and black, I've been sticking to the country road greys. It's where the out-of-the-spotlight people live, too often with fewer options, but better stories to tell. People like the guy behind the counter, with enough common sense to know where he is.

"Can you show me where we're at?" I spread the map out in front of him. He traces on it with a finger wrapped in a raggedy Band-Aid.

"We're here. You've got this road back a ways that'll take you to the west. It's paved but pretty rough. You could go down further to this red one, two seventy-eight, and you'll be just fine. Pretty country too. Lots of pine."

"Thank you." I stretch out my hand. "You've been very helpful."

I fold the map and turn to go, an over-my-shoulder "and I need all the help I can get."

"Don't us all, brother," eyes bright, a toothy grin. "Don't us all."

There are worse things than being lost. I sail across the Atlantic for the first time in 1989 with my friends Dan and Barry. I make a rookie mistake by letting their work deadlines override an ominous weather forecast. We get our brains beat out when a huge Northeasterly rolls over the shoal-riddled shallows off Cape Hatteras. Our boat, aptly named "Outrageous," gets thoroughly swamped, her electrical panel taking a saltwater bath. We lose the primitive Satnav on which we rely for navigation. We've got a difficult decision to make. We have worked for three years in preparation for this trip, and are not inter-ested in turning back.

"We know where we are, our approximate latitude. We can head due east. If the fishermen are white when we get to the other side, we'll turn right. If they're black, we'll turn left. Then follow the big boats into Gibraltar."

Which is stupid, of course, but pretty much what we do after forty-three days at sea. It makes it hard to take seriously any fear of getting lost.

A half hour later I am on a better than average road through southern Arkansas. Telephone poles flash past, trees crowding the road. The sun is where it's supposed to be, dead ahead. Nothing to worry about but the surface beneath me, the critters ready to spring out of the underbrush alongside the road. Nothing to decide but which road I find most interesting at the next junction.

The road is a mix of soft hills and fields as flat as central Illinois. Sweet smelling bales of harvested hay alternate with odorless cotton wrapped in dayglo yellow. Each field is bordered with groves of pine, stately as the white pine that blanketed Michigan in the 1850s, only shorter and slender-trunked. Less threatened also, no burned-down Chicago across the water with its insatiable demand for timber.

A fox lopes across the road ahead, calling me to attention. No, it's too big to be a fox. Are there coyotes down here in Arkansas?

Eyes on the road, John. Take a break if you can't stay focused. I can't. I pull off onto a wide gravel shoulder under a string of oak trees. I take off my jacket to walk around. I am in front of a decrepit old farmhouse, abandoned from the looks of it, hedged in by a fence around a sprawling field of cotton. A screen door hangs from an obstinate hinge beneath broken windows and a dangling shutter. A padlocked chain straddles the driveway entrance. A rusted pickup slouches out beside the partially collapsed barn.

It might have been a beauty once, a woman on the porch and a man, children scampering around the yard, a dog. No longer. The impatience of time, impermanence, accretion. Unstoppable.

Like life itself — my life — the sheer velocity of it. Out of the dark earth we erupt for a brief leafy season, then November crowds in.

Most of the time I am okay with it. But not always.

I can ride, but only so far. Why not relish the history that rides with me, cherish it while I can?

I read somewhere that when Monet's sight was failing in his later years, he went back to many of his flowered canvases and added color to offset his visual loss. Why not take out my own bright colors and lather up these remaining years?

Arkansas is burning up.

Even with the relief of acceleration, sweat is running down my chest, soaking the inside of my vented jacket. I am having trouble keeping a clear head. I barely avoid a huge black snake slithering onto the road, braking and drifting out and around him. Fortunately he stops to let me pass.

I push on, an afternoon-long procession down pine

lined corridors through fields of cotton and corn and hay and soybeans and more cotton. I slow to a crawl through speed restricted towns, heat evacuated into emptiness, their low-hanging roofs and shaded porches, flag waving clotheslines, gas stations and used car lots, faceless burger joints, Dollar Generals and boarded up strip malls, court-houses and churches and cemeteries. And everywhere, high school football field signage, the "Cyclones" or "Dragons" or "Rangers." Then I'm back out onto the pine strung artery to the next overcooked town.

I am wilting again, in need of another stop.

I back off the throttle and drift into a rundown party store with a gas pump outside. I put the kickstand down and sit there, drained, then pull off my helmet and work my way out of my drenched jacket. I wouldn't wear it if I hadn't promised Barbara and the kids I'd keep it on in all conditions this side of impossible. This heat is right up next to impossible.

An ancient pickup rattles to a stop across from me. The door complains when the driver muscles it open. He tumbles down off the driver's seat and steadies himself, much as I am. He's a tough looking old bird, tattoos running up under his chin, sinewy arms dangling from a sleeveless Razorback sweatshirt. He squints suspicion.

I go about my business, unlocking and removing the cap from my gas tank. I take the nozzle from the single blend pump and begin to fill the tank.

When I look up, he's wandered over, more interested in the Honda than its rider.

"Haven't seen one of these for a while."

"Yah, she's an oldster, ninety-five."

"A real beauty," he warms, stepping back for a better look. He breaks into a toothless grin and a barrage of technical questions, most of which I cannot answer. He clearly knows a lot more than I do. He insists on holding my bike upright so I can check the oil level through the window beneath the engine. I thank him and shake his hand.

"Real nice talking with you."

"You too, Sonny" all the squint smiled out of his eyes. "Now I've gotta go pee."

There's nobody behind the counter when I walk in. No air conditioning either. A dog in the corner lifts his head, roused enough to give me a sleepy look over. He's not about to stand up.

"How you doing, Jake?" to which he does not reply.

I walk down an aisle of candy and canned goods to fetch two bottles of water from the cooler. I stand in front of the open door long enough to fog up the glass. When I return to the counter a large woman, face and front shiny with sweat, makes a good-faith effort to smile at me.

"Warm one," she grimaces, then smiles again.

"Tell me."

We're washed out but trying.

"Evelyn!" A man's voice through the screened window behind her. She looks at me, eyes wide, and takes a deep breath.

"Evelyn!"

She whirls and ducks down, face up close to the screen.

"Don't you be hollering at me, Raymond!" with a ferocity that has me stepping back.

Raymond knows better than to answer.

She turns back to me, wags her head, almost curtsies and smiles like a nine-year-old.

"Sorry." And when I say nothing, "thinks he's King fucking Kong."

I chuckle and pay, but she can't let it go.

"He's decent enough" and a wink, "but not much in bed."

More than I need to know. As I thank her and turn to go, another wag of her head and a willowy summation.

"Maybe that's why he barks so much."

I walk out to my bike, nodding, the absurdity of equating book learning and brains.

I head down the road through a heat-dulled procession of cornfields and pine, small towns sweltering under the late afternoon sun. An old woman irons clothes out on her sagging front porch. A log-hauler roars by, wood-chips streaming like locusts off his diesel-spewing truck. There's a faint whiff of sewage at a small-town intersection, the almost aromatic smell of fresh manure off a field further on. There's no break from the heavy heat, almost wet, like sweat.

I am more befuddled than usual at the next junction. I guess left, but don't know why, pull into the parking lot of a small Catholic Church and stop.

I roll my head around to work the stiffness out of my neck. I move my chin back and forth to relieve the tension in my jaw. I have a tightness in my chest. I reach into the front pocket of my jeans and finger the tiny bottle of nitro I keep there. Just knowing it is there helps, thin insurance against an attack.

When my heart settles down, I circle the empty parking lot and pull up alongside a dusty Chevrolet idling under a tree. I shut off the engine and engage the white-haired man behind the wheel.

"Hot one."

"Try on one of these," he grins, gesturing at the roman collar he is wearing.

"I did, a long time ago." I leave it there, too broiled for conversation.

I ask for directions, "something that angles down into Louisiana."

"I am terrible at directions," he apologizes, then makes his case. He rounds off a largely unintelligible set of guesses with a smiling "I hope I've helped you" before setting off on his next priestly errand. He pauses at the end of the driveway for an uncomfortable moment. He clicks on his left turn signal and turns right.

I turn left minutes later, more instinct than conviction. I cross what must be an unmarked border into Louisiana, past signs touting local football teams named after the LSU Tigers. I roll through small towns with their stop sign intersections, grocery stores, gas stations and laundromats. I pass an overgrown graveyard, stones all akimbo, no fence but a padlocked gate.

Flatland farms eventually give way to lush undergrowth and woodlots, greener by the mile. I can smell marshland but see nothing resembling a bayou.

A siren screams in the distance, the boxy strobe-lit ambulance eventually cresting a rise and crowding me onto the soft shoulder of the road. I almost lose control swiveling back onto the asphalt. I am okay, but do not feel okay. Am I losing my nerve?

I pull into a gasoline superstation next to an expressway entrance. I top off the tank and walk inside in search of a restroom and something cold to drink.

The air-conditioned luxury of the place takes over, and a display case full of Krispy Kreme doughnuts. I eat one, chase it with milk, then another, sugar glazed with a chocolate jacket. Then an iced coffee and a People magazine someone left on a table. Who's doing whom, and why do I care?

I finally pry myself away, visions of sleeping bags and snakes.

The sun is flirting with the horizon. I take a deserted two-laner that runs west alongside the freeway. It is pitted but passable, and away from the roar of Sunday night traffic. The heat is tapering as the sun descends, becoming almost pleasant. Relaxed and refreshed, I throttle back for the sheer joy of riding.

A flock of geese appear from out of the north and quack by in almost perfect formation. It seems early to be headed south, but who am I to tell them otherwise.

I hear the growl of a corn harvester out in the fields at twilight. Game birds flushed out ahead of it circle back and land behind to dine on ground-up leftovers. Further back a teenage future farmer straggles along, a burlap bag over his shoulder. He is learning from the ground up, scooping up cobs the harvester missed.

I pass a flock of black chickens milling along the unfenced side of the road. Would I even see them a half hour from now? And the deer, up and moving now, focused only on dinner at dusk.

I take the next ramp onto the highway, hoping to pile up some deer-free miles before dark. I work my way into a hornets' nest of cars and trucks, a Sunday night swarm back toward Texas. It is everything I go out of my way to avoid. A long procession of semis own the right lane, too big to care much about the midgets hurtling by on the left. I tuck in between two of the big guys for a while, buffeted by tailwinds off the one in front, too aware of the one behind. I struggle to keep my bike from shuddering in the cross currents they generate. No good. I accelerate into a gap between tinted-window pickups in the passing lane. These boys are in a caffeinated fever, blazing up into the nineties when they have the room to run. They nuzzle up behind any vehicle going slower, flashing their brights, swerving in and out between trucks, squeezing in where they can. Another place I do not want to be.

I ease back into the right lane after passing a long string of trucks, open road for as far as I can see. I can breathe again.

It is dark by the time I pass a sign announcing Texas. I come up behind a U-haul taking his time. I check behind me, swing out and around, then glide back into the right lane and throttle down. I glance into my cracked rearview mirror and see a pair of headlights closing fast from behind. A black Dodge Charger thunders by, hits the brights then the brakes, slowing enough that the U-Haul and I come up alongside him. Surprised, I glance over at him, easy enough because he switches on an overhead light. Someone is slouched down in the seat beside him, head up against the window.

I touch the brakes lightly, expecting he will take off again. He doesn't. Instead he drifts over toward me. I honk, but he does not even look up from the cellphone he has pinned against the steering wheel. I shout my alarm as if he could hear me, and he continues to slide, crowding me out to the far edge of my lane. He keeps coming, wheels up next to me. I brake and swerve to the right to avoid him, out on the asphalt apron now, wobbling, almost fishtailing, regaining some control and skidding to a stop just short of the roadside ditch.

The Charger has veered back into his lane and hammered it, giving the U-haul room to squeeze by between us. Then he rockets off, not even a hesitation. The U-haul driver slows long enough to see that I am upright, headlight angling out into the underbrush. Then he too is gone, taillights trailing off into the night.

I muscle my bike up onto the apron, reach down and pat the tank.

"Thank you, my friend. You saved my ass."

I point the front tire in the right direction before the next caravan of trucks rumbles up. I switch on my caution lights, just sit there and breathe, hiccups and gasps at first, then longer breaths punctuated by gulps. My heart is racing, pulse pounding, the vague suggestion of a headache. I am trembling. I put down the kickstand and climb off, try to shake the quivering out of my arms. I stretch my legs and walk around.

That was way too close.

Pressure is welling up in my chest, the dark beginning of a spasm. I get the nitro out of my pocket and slip a first bitter pill under my tongue. The pain begins to ease after I take a second.

The next wave of trucks roll up. They flash their brights and thunder by like cars on a passing train. An SUV pulls off the road ahead of me and stops. I shout assurance to the driver walking back toward me.

"I am okay. Just taking a break."

He pauses, waves, and turns back.

"Thank you for stopping."

Just being stopped could cause an accident. I take a deep breath and climb back on my bike. I slip on my helmet, tighten the chin strap and pop up the visor to defog it. My hands are no longer shaking.

I turn the key and hit the ignition. The engine and the headlight come to life. I wait for a gap between the passing trucks, swing out and throttle down hard.

Emotional equilibrium returns with the miles. I am parched and starving as the stress subsides, and dead-dog tired. I get off at the first exit with signage for restaurants and turn in at a truck stop that promises "Good Food and Cheap." I shed my helmet and jacket at the fuel pump, and begin to fill the tank. The sodium lights give the place an otherworld air, the odor of diesel fuel, the idling engines, the movement of women among the parked rigs. Life on the long road at the end of the day.

Drivers are slouched sideways on the settees of several booths in the restaurant, dozing over the remains of all-you-can-eat dinners. I sit on a hardback chair at a table, to support my aching back.

A gray-haired man enters a few minutes later and moves to the table in front of me. He runs his hands under the back of his pleated slacks as he eases onto the chair, no sense getting wrinkled.

"No need for a menu, honey" when the waitress sets a glass of ice water in front of him. "Just give me the usual, and a strong cup of coffee." She nods with pursed lips and a squint, moves by him to hand me a menu.

"A very strong cup of coffee" he bellows as she retreats to the kitchen.

"Very strong" again, after she disappears, and chuckles to himself. He cranes his head around to where a wakened driver glares at him.

"Well enough of that" in the same honeyed drawl, then goes silent until the waitress returns.

She approaches him tentatively, puts a cup of coffee down in front of him from the far side of the table.

"Why thank you, sweetie" with the same saccharin familiarity. She says nothing, and moves silently around him to take my order.

"How's the lasagna?"

"A favorite of the regulars," she says. "Probably *the* favorite."

"That's good enough for me. And a Diet Coke, please." She takes the menu, and moves on to a driver gesturing for his bill.

She's right about the lasagna. I polish it off and use two baseball-size dinner rolls to erase any evidence of sauce from my plate.

Most of the truckers have settled up and left during my feeding frenzy. The wavy-haired lothario at the next table stays, dousing himself with coffee. He does everything possible to get himself backhanded by the waitress. She seems more than capable of holding him at bay, her disdain open if unspoken.

As his frustration mounts, an almost attacking "cat got your tongue?" as she turns her back and walks toward the kitchen.

"Hey, Mister" – I cannot help myself – and "Hey, Mister" again when he does not turn. This time he swivels around.

"Maybe that's enough." And when he doesn't reply, "She doesn't seem to be enjoying your attention."

This is something he's not used to, I guess. He says nothing, just turns away.

He keeps his peace when the waitress returns, only snaps his credit card down on the table. He signs hurriedly when she comes back and tosses the pen down in front of her. He stands up abruptly and moves towards the door with an over-the-shoulder "chin up, sugar," to which she replies with an unwaitressy "Asshole."

I nod my support when she walks over.

"Thank you," she says, shaking her head, letting herself get angry.

"He owns the biggest car dealership around here," blood rising in her neck and cheeks.

"Gets all stirred up at the 'gentlemen's club' – that's what they call it – down the road, then parks his lard ass in here and gets all lovey-dovey with anyone willing to wait on him."

I nod again. She needs to be heard.

"Anyway, thank you," and she walks away, "that scum bucket!" the last thing out of her mouth.

She returns minutes later, takes my bill and credit card off to the cash register. I glance down at the Joseph Campbell quote I carry in my open billfold.

"The goal is to live
With Godlike composure
On the full rush of energy,
Like Dionysus riding the leopard,
Without being torn to pieces."

I am back on the expressway, anything but composed, the Dodge Charger crowding in.

I get a room at the first motel I come to, a better brand than I am used to. I kick off my boots and flop in a swivel chair to study a list of available channels. I decide against turning on the TV, a too obvious escape from unsettledness.

I take out my billfold and open again to the Joseph Campbell quote. I am back in the living room of a university guest house with him and a handful of fawning academics. In the course of the afternoon sunlight makes its way across the Persian rug to his sturdy shoes, up his corduroy pantlegs, and into his lap. He is an old man and still talking, sharing time and ideas as if he doesn't have to speak this evening. His eyes sparkle as he gestures, the baritone enthusiasm of an 80-year-old child. He is almost iridescent, energy and passion that years cannot erase.

Why not live like that?

Not the *torn to pieces* part. I flirted with that out on the freeway, the difference between extension and risk. Whatever banner I hang on it, stupid is still stupid.

But the *full rush of energy*, less like a tourist in the only life I have. A deeper attention in these dwindling moments to what might otherwise go unattended. The waitress tonight and the worn-out truckers, the guy in the pleated slacks. A less guarded participation in the life we share, unblinkered, dark and light.

CHAPTER 8

I GOT in too late last night to call Barbara. I reach her by phone during my first cup of coffee. She fills me in on her day and updates me on the kids. Everybody seems to be doing well. I tell her about last night's misadventure in a matter-of-fact voice, complete with assurances of lessons learned.

She listens without a belabored commentary on safety, apparently confident I have connected the dots.

"You still having fun?"

"Yup, in spite of yesterday's drama. I love the back-road beauty of the South, out-of-the-way people in their out-of-the-way towns. It's everything I'd hoped for."

"Well, soak it up, Johnny Bob, and bring it back home."

"Safely," I assure her.

"I know you will."

She used the same words – "I know you will" – on the last phone conversation we had almost thirty years ago, the night before I sailed out of Morocco to cross the Atlantic alone. I had just assured her – and myself – that I was going to be okay.

When she replied "I know you will," I realized that I did too.

A light morning drizzle begins to fall while I am fastening my tank bag to the bike. Fear has taken up residence in my body, that vague intersection between caution and paralysis. I know the first minutes of rain are the most dangerous, capable of turning oil on the road into a slippery grease.

I opt for another cup of coffee and the morning paper, time enough for even a mild rain to wash the worst of the oil off the pavement. I nibble at a chocolate chip muffin I do not need for the comfort it provides.

Heightened attention please, less the dread.

I climb on my bike and hit the starter. The engine growls, then steadies. I let it idle while zipping up the air vents on my rain jacket. I work wet fingers down into my gloves, cinch my helmet strap tighter than is comfortable. I retract the kickstand, throttle up slightly, ease out across the parking lot onto the road.

I ride tight for the first miles, rigid in even the

mildest curves, getting the feel of the road. I relax some-what as the city miles spool out into the countryside, even more when I find an agreeable two-laner. The soft rain persists, warm but still lethal. Because most of the oil resides in the strip between tire-worn grooves, I pick a track and stick with it, the one least likely to let go of a tire.

I want to be safe. I don't want to let exaggerated fear ring the joy out of this wet Texas morning.

I've only wiped out once in my life, on a bridge over the Mississippi forty years ago. My small-bore tire found a groove in an angled railroad track that probably shouldn't have been in service. A lot of rolling and scraping and banging around in the pitch black 3:00 A.M. I was out of the hospital soon after dawn, but with a bike so broken I couldn't complete my first cross-country run.

One crash is more than enough.

I'm settling in nicely when a shiny black Land Rover blows by me. Startled, I glance in my rearview mirror just as the circus lights flash on above a trailing patrol car. He jets by me with a siren beep and a sheet of spray and escorts his prey to the shoulder of the road. It is a routine I was familiar with a long time ago, this time with another guy in the starring role.

The rain gives way to thin cloud cover and then to an ardent sun. This is Texas hill country, forests yielding to green undulations speckled with small and not-so-small ranches. Cattle country. Lush green knolls and

wide-open spaces, not a hint of the Midwest's soybeans
and corn. Grass mostly, and lots of cows.

I use the gas gauge as an excuse to stop at a shiny superstation. A gangly teenage boy is standing out front while
I fill up, toe-tapping his restlessness with red and black
high tops. He glances at me and walks away, hauling up
his oversized shorts every third step.

I grab a bottle of water from the cooler inside and
wait in line behind an over-leathered cowboy. When we
finally reach the cash register he grabs the edge of the
counter and asks for "today's Wall Street Journal" with
almost military authority. When he gets nothing but the
clerk's vacant stare, he shakes his head in disbelief.
Nobody speaks. After a few tense seconds, he lets loose
of the counter edge, whirls, scowls at the rest of us, and
stomps out the door. Everyone turns to watch him climb
up into his truck and slam the door. The clerk and I look
at each other, nod, say nothing.

Two young men flick their cigarettes out into the
parking lot as they shoulder past me in the doorway.

"Let's get us a twelve-pack and resolve this once and
for all."

The fields go from green to bone colored in central Texas. The sun has vanquished morning's humidity, the countryside more austere in the midday heat. Even the most obstinate underbrush retreats to gullied breaks in the landscape. What green there is resides behind ornate fencing, country estates with grand signage over their entrances. Places where underground sprinklers make up for infrequent rain.

The world begins to turn green again as I approach the sprawl around Austin. Lush lawns, white fences, and school buses now, watering holes for the commuter set and fastfood joints for the rest of us. No stomach for rush hour traffic, I stop for a pool-size chocolate shake at a refrigerated McDonald's. I go back to my bike to get a book. As inviting as the grass looks under a tree next to the parking lot, the purgatorial heat drives me back inside.

Young mothers are rolling in with their children for an afterschool snack. Rather than diving into my book, I spool back to Barbara's "still having fun?" on the phone this morning. I assured her I was, but am I?

I claim to love venturing out beyond my comfortable world into the more rigorous unknown. How compelling it sounds in a quiet room or crowded auditorium, microphone in hand.

How about here, right now? Drenched, then baked and bone-weary.

The gift of adventure or a hyper-fraught slog?

I alone decide the eyes I bring to it, and with circumstance fashion my life.

An hour later I am on a through-town expressway with those feverish boys and their trucks. They are the kings of the road down here, or at least the left lane of any road they travel. Hang on tight if they catch you out there, no matter how hard you're pushing. They will do everything but mount you from behind until you submit to a slower lane. And if you take too long, some maniac will roar by in a cloud of exhaust and swerve in ahead of you, just so you know. I get off at the first exit with a sign for a budget motel.

I carry my gear up to a second-floor room, too used up to think about taking a walk. Like a day at the helm in the aroused Atlantic or breaking up sidewalks between semesters at school. I collapse on a lumpy mattress without removing my boots.

I wake up at dusk and check my Fitbit, still time for dinner and a walk. I am in Austin, Texas. The night is young. I'll rest later.

I wash the dust off my face and force a comb through my matted hair. You go with what you've got. Soon I am out on the street looking for a Margarita and a plate of something good, a tonic for my depletion.

The hostess seems less than ecstatic at my arrival. She takes her time cross-checking the available tables against the crayoned plastic diagram taped to the podium.

She smiles broadly at something a waiter whispers as he passes by.

She has very white teeth, crooked and brilliant, and eyes as grey as a wolf. She grabs a menu, a pursed-lip exhalation, and escorts me through a maze of boisterous diners to a table along the wall.

"Can I get you something to start?" while leaning away to grab the wrist of a retreating busboy.

"Just water, please."

She moves on, no sign of hearing.

It takes a long time for a waiter to arrive and ask again. I order a Margarita and a glass of water, squeeze in an order of garlic shrimp. He may not be back for a while.

I have been telling myself I love being anonymous, the freedom a visitor feels in a foreign land. It's a carry-over from years as an elected official, the unsolvable tension between promised availability and the privacy I desired.

This feels different, like not mattering enough to even register in the eyes of people I pass. I tell myself it's just my frail male ego, a perfect antidote to the small-orbit stardom I took too seriously in the past. That's certainly part of it. What Leonard Cohen was referring to when he playfully described men's stages of aging as "relevance, irrelevance, invisibility, disgusting, and cute."

This feels like invisibility to me, a tepid male version of the real distress too many women experience as they age. It's one more reason to look others in the eye, attention they deserve.

Then again, I could be in denial. Perhaps I'm in the incipient stage of "disgusting", or worse. Is "sweetie" a term reserved for old men who are "cute"?

———

Mercifully a sizzling plate of shrimp arrives to break the fever of self-absorption. I dive in with a zeal only my dog, Finnegan, would appreciate. Or my father, whose grace in decline suggests grace is possible.

I give the waiter a credit card when he stops by with the bill. He returns my card, and sets an iPad down on the table in front of me. I look up at him with the befuddlement I saw too often in my students' eyes.

"Just the total," pointing to a box on the screen, "and sign your name down below."

"Do you have a pen?"

His eyes widen.

"No pen on these, Sir. Just use your finger." He waves his finger to show me how.

I do not tell him that I have recently graduated from a number two pencil to a ballpoint pen. I take a run at it, finger on the screen, a spastic scrawl.

I hand the iPad back to him, smile, and assure him I will leave a cash tip. He smiles back and retreats, an episode he will undoubtedly share later.

I stop at the restroom on my way out, only discovering several crowded blocks later that I have left my fly unzipped.

Invisibility does have its rewards.

CHAPTER 9

I'VE HAD JUST a taste of Austin. I want more.

Over coffee in the morning, I use my fancy iPhone to track down a bookstore friends back home have raved about. Google calls up an address and a map, amazing what these things can do.

Within an hour I am wandering around "Book People" with an armful of books and the weekend newspaper. I buy the newspaper and head for the coffee shop, pay at the counter for coffee and a scone, rent for a table in a world-class bookstore. I wade through the newspaper then narrow my book purchases down to two, hoping to find room for them on my bike.

During a long wait in the checkout line, I overhear a tense discussion between the people behind me.

"I've got to watch it. They're threatening to garnish my wages."

"And you're buying those magazines?"

"I'm not going to pay for them. I'm putting them on my card."

Let me out of here.

It is sunny outside, but not the furnace heat of the last several days.

I find room on my bike for one of the books and take the other with me on a hike to the University of Texas campus. I can't find the bookstore in spite of some earnest directions, and settle onto a bench in the student café to read and cool off.

I spend more than an hour on the open mall beneath the tower from which Charles Whitman targeted students during his murderous mass shooting in the sixties. It was the first of what has become commonplace these days. I walk away with renewed distress at the fragility of the human psyche, the pain and rage so many carry.

I want relief. Walking back through the campus in the now sweltering heat, I come across a fountain and beyond it a pond.

I try to let Charles Whitman go.

If there is brutality, there is beauty also, the sound of water, children playing with their parents, their antics on the wall that circles the pond.

Further on young lovers sprawl in a single lawn chair, her fingers up along his neck.

Am I not supposed to notice?

Must seven decades wall off the delicacy of fingers, the fine line of a wrist?

I am seventy-four, old enough – wise or worn down – to care less.

I do not care less.

I have no interest in getting over what others consider the purview of the young — not the objectification or the longing to possess, but the pure nourishment that beauty affords. As age slows me down, I see more and feel.

———

I call Barbara and tell her about my day. She reminds me that the Whitman massacre occurred almost sixty years ago. We decide to leave it there. On my walk and its beauty she only chuckles.

"That sounds a lot more like you than this talk of carnage. I'd focus there."

When we end our conversation, I go on walking. A stoplight signals activity at a corner, a bar and restaurant, a bookstore with dated books on a table out front. I can't help myself, stopping to thumb my way into titles I do not recognize. A book about Picasso grabs my attention, his interesting take on aging: "It takes a lot of time to become young," a line that walks with me to a table down the street.

"Become as little children" comes to mind over a

mountain of guacamole and a sour-tasting amber. What is young if not an open mind and heart, a capacity for wonder? A natural state to the unbruised child, a long trek back for those of us with a lot to let go of. Hurt and hesitation if life has been harsh. Caution and over-calculation, the endless strategizing to stay safe or gain advantage. Raw fear in some instances, an overwrought readiness to react or attack. A lot to reckon with on the road back to young.

The breeze feels good when I motor back to the motel. I retreat to the air-conditioned room to pull gear together for morning's ride to the west.

I should turn in, but I'm not ready to sleep. I step back into the oven outside, check my Fitbit, then set out on a walk through an aging entertainment district. It's a bit rundown, rap and country cranked up high, voices also, laughter.

It doesn't take long to get steamed up, finish today's four miles.

I turn back toward the motel when the yawns kick in. I come up to a man sitting on a doorstep, scrawny dog and a cardboard sign, an uneven but direct "I need some help." I reach for my billfold to relieve him of making a pitch. I am also buying my way out of staying longer, the attention more valuable than a drop in the bucket.

As I walk further, I drift back to Spain, the spring of

2001. Barbara and I are there with our two youngest children, time off the ocean on our sailboat, *Grace*. We are stern-anchored in the Guadalquivir River on the last day of Feria, Seville's weeklong celebration of their beloved horses.

A man takes off his clothes and shoes during the night. He leaves them in an orderly pile on a bridge walkway, then throws himself in the river below. We hear nothing, although we are less than a hundred yards away. We only learn of him when the police begin dragging the river in the morning.

How many people are standing on that dark bridge tonight, a few minutes of attention between them and despair?

My heart knots up as I walk, a weight in my chest that slows me to a crawl. It eases somewhat when I stop to brace myself against a pickup truck, then ratchets up a block further on. I put a nitro under my tongue and I stand in a doorway waiting for it to kick in. It buys me some relief on the way back to the motel.

I come to a full stop on the stairway up to my room. I try to be cool, as the kids might say. I am not cool. I am far from Barbara and the kids. The west Texas flats are waiting out ahead. It is almost midnight and still up in the eighties.

I am not even close to cool.

CHAPTER 10

THE WORLD DOESN'T END VERY OFTEN.

I dive deep during an air-conditioned night, waking when a maid knocks on the door at eleven.

"Got to clean the room, Mister, unless you're staying over." I have opened the door a crack and am standing naked behind it. I glance out over her shoulder into the already torrid parking lot.

"Could you tell them downstairs that I've decided to stay over?"

"Happy to do so, Mister," and a broad smile. "One less room to clean."

———

I have devoured days and am grateful for their nourishment. I want to savor this bonus day in Austin. More than a reprieve, it's a luxury — time to linger over breakfast and a newspaper, a long walk to look around.

By midafternoon I am back at my now favorite table in the coffee shop at "Book People," sifting through a pile of books. The place fills up gradually, students mostly, clicking away at their keyboards and checking their phones. It's easy to feel old in Austin.

Age doesn't seem like a burden today, more a source of entertainment. After last night's cardiac adventure, I am delighted to be old and alive. I order a bagel with cream cheese, a coffee on the side. It feels like a celebration.

I saunter through the university district later, a renewed appreciation for the drumbeat of years, birthday signposts with their accelerating numbers, decades compressed into single candles. The sheer silliness of keeping count. None of it should be shocking, but the pace of aging is shocking.

What to do with seventy-four?

Denial doesn't work. Whining is a particularly despicable form of self-debasement, the bankruptcy of victimhood. Besides, it's just embarrassing.

I claim to relish challenge, the lure of the unknown. It's time to come to terms with what's right in front of me. A damaged heart and a faltering aortic valve, a handful of pills morning and night. A stiff back and complaining right hip, less strength than I had before. A bleeder now and slow to heal, reading glasses that get thicker every year. A dictatorial prostate with its night-time demands, those wide-awake hours before dawn. Hair gone white and thinning. The list goes on. If these were glacial changes at first, I'm in avalanche territory now. That's not piling on. That's reality.

None of it demands unnecessary concessions, giving up on an intense and passionate life. An honest account is different from surrender. I can shorten my reach without giving up reaching, reef my sails without reefing my life.

CHAPTER 11

RUSH HOUR TRAFFIC provides an excuse to eat a
full breakfast at a restaurant near campus. I have no
desire to dance with trucks on the freeway. The
morning paper does little to energize, however much
energy would help today.

I fold up the paper and put it aside, gaze out the bay
window, a second cup of coffee. Students hurry by on
the sidewalk outside, backpacks and books and morning
resolve. I need some of that resolve to offset the hesitation I feel about the stifling heat of the west Texas
desert. Today's forecast ranges between ninety and one
hundred and five, and it's getting hotter each minute I
wait.

I pay, check tire pressure and oil, and mount up. I
am less than a mile down the still crowded expressway
when a station wagon swerves in front of me to avoid a
tire in the middle of his lane. I swing to the far edge of

my lane, hugging the line, slowing enough to avoid his back bumper without getting clobbered from behind. It works.

It's not the call to attention I was looking for, but it certainly does the trick.

I get off at the first exit that announces a road to the west. There's still a lot of morning action on the two-laner through suburbs overrun with arriving boomers. Everything is green for a while, lawns and pastures, golf courses with their whirling sprinklers. A collective amnesia about the aridity that created these open spaces, as if there were no limit to the aquifers beneath.

The suburbs yield to well-attended ranches, horses and cattle alike. Out beyond a bright white fence a blond woman in riding britches reaches down to stroke the shiny black neck of her riding companion. She hears me coming, turns, and stares as I whirl by. She does not wave when I nod.

Out beyond the fields and bottomlands, the bluffs give way to cardboard-colored flatlands and bone-dry basins where rivers once ran. I pass occasional feedlots the size of football fields and larger. I can smell them for miles before I see them. They haunt me for hours after I pass. Pay attention, John, to what you'd rather not see.

The scent of oil hangs in the overcooked air, from

rigs within easy reach of the road. Their mechanical arms arch and plunge, black money from barren ground.

The road straightens out and flattens, an occasional wide curve, then straight and flat some more. Two cars approach me from out of the distance, closing in a hurry. I flash my brights when one moves into my lane to pass. He keeps on coming, apparently oblivious, then swerves back in just before I'd have to bail out.

Breathe, Johnny Boy. Breathe.

The asphalt beneath me is simmering now, the oily odor gathering in my sweat-soaked jeans and the crash-padded jacket I promised to wear. I throttle up to create a breeze where none exists. It helps, but not enough to stave off dehydration.

I stop for gas and air conditioning the next chance I get. I turn my drenched jacket inside out and sling it over the handlebars. I go inside and get a bottle of water from the cooler. I begin to gulp it, almost bumping into the hunched-over old man behind me at the counter.

"Oops, I'm sorry."

He's taken some hits, his face a handful of mismatched parts. He has light in his pale blue eyes.

"What's that ya ridin?" he asks but doesn't seem all that interested when I tell him. Only nods.

"Used to drive a Harley myself, till they made me get off."

"That's not right," I grin, and shake my head.

He straightens up as much as he can.

"I'd go back there if I could." No whine, just matter-of-fact.

Back at my bike, I reluctantly pull on my jacket. It's hot, but you keep your word. Like the old man inside, my father's generation. Take what life gives you, no need for complaint, suck it up and carry on.

I've certainly got nothing to complain about. I'm exactly where I want to be, doing what I want to do. This sweltering road, these ignited miles. A cold beer when I get there.

I pass a gigantic surface mine operation. There's only an occasional green tainted field now, scattered trees, cattle huddled around a pump-fed pond. Grassland replaced by patches of scrub brush, mostly in gullies, faint promise of water if a storm cloud bursts. Survival seems less likely for their unprotected companions, leaking life under the punishing sun.

Green disappears entirely in time, its perspective-giving contours. It's all tableland now, bleached and dry, soil to sand to dust. A place to die, life baked off the bones. As Cormac McCarthy put it, "no country for old men."

It gets harder to focus as the temperature rises, burning away my flagging resolve. I would welcome the sight of any being — car, truck, cow, anything. The sameness of the road and emptiness of the desert nudge me beyond sluggishness towards stupor. I don't want to doze off and startle awake when it's too late to matter.

Through the waves of radiating heat, there's something vertical up the road. Reality or mirage? I shake my head to clear it. Something in the shimmer, a sign, no, a building.

Water?

Air conditioning?

I pull in next to a gas pump, just sit there, gathering myself. I remember stopping at a rundown gas station in the California desert on my first cross country motorcycle run in 1971. I swung my leg over my 350cc and collapsed onto my hands and knees.

I thought I knew hot.

I did not know hot like this.

I climb off my bike and steady myself, peel off my jacket and helmet. I somehow manage to overfill the tank and look for some paper towels to wipe up the overflow. There are no paper towels, nor gas for that matter, sucked up by the sun-crusted ground. I walk over to the station and enter. It's light on supplies, but an air-conditioned upgrade from the furnace outside.

I make my way to a modest cooler and gulp down the first of several bottles of water. I call out a replenished "hello." There's no reply. More water, a more robust "hello," still no answer. I go back to the water, a third saturated "hello." Nothing. I turn away from the cooler and am startled to find her standing behind me.

"A little patience, please," in an even voice, a very thin "please."

"I'm sorry. I was concerned that nobody was here."

"I'm here," the same steely cadence.

Small talk is out.

She lumbers to the counter to cash me out. I'm nowhere near cool enough to hurry back outside. I set my empty bottles on the counter to assure her.

"If it's okay with you, I'm going to look around." The same impassive eyes. "Probably get something else."

Nothing, not even a nod.

I am done with repentance. I go back to the cooler and open the door to a luxurious blast. I take my time checking the fancy iced coffees, pick one and take it to the counter.

I return to the cooler for a small carton of milk, check the freshness date and take it to the counter.

She watches me closely, neither moves nor speaks.

I take the bottled coffee with me when I pick my way through a sunscreen display. I choose an S-P 70 even though I have a small tube of sunblock on my bike.

"I think that'll do it," to which she does not reply. She punches the cash register like hammering nails and pushes the paper bill across the counter.

I pay in cash to avoid her expected disapproval if I

take out my credit card. I figure I've purchased enough to rent more time in the air conditioning. I take my loot over to a trash container near the door, deposit the empties and place the rest on its flat plastic top. I open the milk and take a gulp, then go back to the coffee.

She sits on a stool behind the counter. She is watching every time I look over.

The thermometer under the awning outside registers one hundred and three. And there's no awning out on the asphalt. It hardens my resolve to stay where I am until I've cooled off some more. I reckon I paid for it. I throw the empty bottles in the trash when I finish and walk back to the restroom.

I splash cold water on my face, neck and arms. I stand under the air conditioning vent for as long as I can and flush the unused toilet. I walk back through the store and out to my bike to get a thermos. The afternoon is on fire. I walk back to the bathroom to fill it.

She has not moved a bit during my comings and goings. I have a grudging respect for her almost catatonic discipline, not a strong suit of mine. She's like an ill-tempered desert Buddha, message to be teased out when I am back on the road. I am not going to get myself killed out there. I will stop for the night the next chance I get. Until then, it's grip hard and hold the line.

I twist the top off the sunscreen and I lather up my forearms for the first time since leaving. I've decided not to put my jacket back on and will bungee it to the road bag that rides behind me. Wearing it seems more dangerous than riding unprotected. I will explain to Barbara and the kids later. They will understand or not.

It's hard to draw a full breath when I go back outside, like breathing in an oven. The motorcycle is too hot to sit on, the handlebars almost blistering to the touch. The clerk has disappeared when I walk back through the store to the bathroom. I lock the door, remove my t-shirt, and fill the sink with cold water. I douse my shirt, leather gloves, and a bandana I have not used.

I remove a wad of paper towels from the dispenser, soak them, and fashion them into a layered wet seat. I hope it will allow me to ride. I ring out the t-shirt and put it on, gloves and bandana when I get back to the bike. I climb over and settle onto my paper towel seat. It seems to work. I put on my helmet, retract the kickstand, turn the key and hit the ignition.

The drenched t-shirt and seat work for fifty miles, aided by the airflow around me. I simmer rather than seethe. The sunscreen on my forearms cooks to a greasy crust as I ride, flakes burning off like the heat shield of a returning spacecraft.

Reality warps into a shimmering apparition in the afternoon heat. Like life itself, everything an oscillation. It gets difficult to see in the glare of the westerly sun. My

attention is dissolving. I need to find somewhere –
anywhere – to stop.

A smudge emerges out on the horizon, in time a
water tower and town. A school bus rolls towards me
from out of the dust. I stop when the lights above it
begin to flash and an automated stop sign pops out. It's
hard to believe all the windows are open. Squeals wash
over me, finger pointing and excitement at the motorcycle man.

Several scrawny dogs bound out from between
mobile homes across the road, barking and romping as
the bus door snaps open. A swarm of boys spill out onto
the side of the road, shouting in Spanish and diving into
the frenzy. A single serious looking girl steps down after
them, acting put off by their rowdiness.

I'm revived by the energy of the children, the
prospect of getting off my bike. Burnout shifts in the
direction of satisfaction. Weary, adolescent, and real.

The bus wheezes and the door jerks shut. The salty
haired woman behind the wheel retracts her stop sign
and clicks off her flashers. The bus lumbers down the
road. I ease around the kids, past the mobile home park
and down the town's main street, awninged store fronts,
a bar, a miniature post office and a police department.
Buildings, but in this scalding sun, no people. I pass a
beauty shop, a prosperous looking bakery, and a
rundown bar. There's a hardware store – always a good
sign – and another bar. Further on there's a restaurant
and two motels, proclaiming air conditioning as if it

were an option. I turn in at the one with a single lawn chair out front, pulled right up to the road. A round faced old woman signs me in and smiles, then seems shocked when I extend my MasterCard.

"One second, please," she stammers, and retreats into the back room.

"Walter," and when he doesn't answer, "Walter" again.

Walter appears at the counter a minute later, hunched over uncomfortably. He has sideburns down to the line of his clenched jaw, pain in his hooded eyes.

"Not that complicated," he sputters. He runs the card and hands me a key.

"Out the door and down to the left," he gestures, and only then looks up to make eye contact. When he does, his hard eyes soften.

"I hope you like it."

"I'm sure I will."

I take my jacket and bike bag down to unit seven. It is clean and pleasant in a 1970s way, and so cold I dial up the temperature setting. Then I am face down on the flowered bedspread.

It is early evening when I open my eyes, the sun blood red through the window blinds next to the bed. I close my eyes and the world disappears. When I open them again, it is dark outside. Where am I? I lift my head and look around. Wherever I am, I have a very sore neck, the revenge of a helmet and an oversized head. I have an ache in my back when I sit up, an engine burn on the inside of my calf. My wrist complains when I reach under the florid lampshade to flick on the bedside lamp.

Just why did I come out here?

My growling stomach gives me a sense of direction. A moth flutters under the bulb housing when I turn on the light in the bathroom. I squeak on the hot water, rusty at first, and notice cigarette burns on the rubber tiles next to the toilet. I look for a washcloth when the water is hot, but settle for the corner of a towel. I rub away at my sunburned face, and when I remove the bandana, my windburned neck. I lather my arms with the well-used bar of soap on the sink, and peel away what's left of the sunblock. I comb my matted hair with my fingers, and – what's the use – give up on further grooming. I'm hungry, and it's moving up on closing time.

It is still oven hot outside, but tolerable without the sun. There are survivors of the afternoon broil on the street now, and the whirl of air conditioners as I pass a crowded bar.

A cluster of high-riding pickups stand in front of an Italian restaurant, a huge tractor trailer and a few aging sedans. Dated music leaks out when someone enters or leaves. I am eager to be around people after a hot and solitary run. This place feels just right.

Two young men bound out of a truck and clamor up

the stairs ahead of me. I squeeze by them when they stop to whisper, "Me and you and all of them losers" in dayglo orange on the back of their shirts. I think better of stopping to ask.

The place is cool and dark inside, black vinyl uphol-stery, an unvarnished wood floor. Bright lights over the bar suggest an emphasis on alcohol over food. No table is lit enough to open a book over dinner. But there are people, a few of whom turn and nod at an unfamiliar face. It feels good, if a bit needy, to be acknowledged after a stint of alone.

I take an empty table close to the bar. I order a draft and dinner from a waitress, who returns with a west Texas draft and a weary smile. The meal itself is slow in coming, time enough to drift back over the decades and out to sea.

I am fifteen days and two thousand miles out of Casablanca, at least ten days away from a Barbados reunion with Barbara and the kids. I am tired and alone, scuffed up from an afternoon shimmy up the mast to retrieve a frayed halyard. I am too weary to prepare dinner and too seasick to eat, already used up, fifteen hundred miles to go. And there's no one to take the wheel so I can sleep, step in if I tumble, come back if I lose balance and fall overboard.

Alone.

It's what you wanted, I remind myself, lessons of solitude and extension. What exhaustion has to teach, raw hands on the wheel, rub-burned arms and legs.

Work with what you've got is a long-held default position when overwhelmed. I have a fifteen knot tradewind and manageable swells. There is no immediate crisis to deal with, only this easy pitch and roll. I have time to rest if not refuel.

With dark I let the stars take over, the soothing rhythm of following seas. Alarm melts away, the claustrophobic sense of separateness.

I am okay.

Revelry ends when something smacks the side of my head. I jerk away instinctively, hand up to ward off my attacker, but there is no attacker. I grab a flashlight and aim it spasmodically around the cockpit. No one, nothing.

Did that really happen? I reach up to the side of my head, am relieved to find a damp spot in my hair.

I redirect the flashlight beam around the cockpit. Still nothing.

Then something flutters beneath me. I twist the flashlight down and find my assailant on the cockpit floor, silver and blue, eyes cartoon-wide, and whirling transparent wings. A flying fish on a midnight run, every bit as surprised as me.

He thrashes away from my first halting attempts to pick him up. He's having none of it. He wrests free of my grasp, wings afrenzy in a stunned attempt to get airborne. He soon weakens, oxygen-starved enough that I can grab his wings and fling him back into the sea. I am left with a scatter of silver scales and the indelible aroma of very fresh fish. Laughter also, and a renewed sense that I am a small part of everything around me.

At sea or out in nowhere Texas, it is impossible to be alone.

———

The waitress returns with a steamy heap of lasagna and the smiled gift of silence. I pick up a fork and shovel the first mouthful of improbably fresh pasta, cheesy sweet and tomato-tart, then follow with a gulp of full-bodied brown beer. Good enough to savor before swallowing.

Between bites I take in the people around me, more vivid for the hours on the road. A stoop-shouldered old timer waddles in, grimacing discomfort as he works his way onto a barstool. His face brightens when the bartender saunters down to greet him.

"How they hangin', Harry?"

"Jumpin' when I see you, Hon."

"Your regular?" These two know each other well.

"Yup, and something to chase it."

She smiles and winks, wiggles her behind just a bit.

"You're the man, Harry."

An elderly woman sits alone two tables away. She tosses her fork onto her plate with a flourish and swabs her face with a napkin. She drops her hands in her lap and studies the empty plate with a flush of accomplishment. She grabs her empty beer bottle off the table, hoists it, and sucks away like a nursing child. She thumps it back down on the table and exhales satisfaction. She reaches the inside of a wrist up under her nose and inhales deeply. She studies Harry at the bar, and smiles.

I turn back to my lasagna, the sudden image of a woman I saw in London. She was standing on a platform across from us in a Tube station, arms tight across the breast of her long gray coat. She was hugging herself, and swaying, a desperate hunger.

When I look up, my aged companion is on her feet and moving across the room to a barstool next to Harry. Harry cranes his neck to glance down her blouse when she turns her attention to the bartender.

"Don't be sneakin' no peeks, Harry," breaking off her conversation and swiveling back to him. "Keep that up and people will start thinkin' you're a pervert."

"Start?" the bartender chimes in.

"Just cuz I'm decrepit don't mean I'm blind!" he protests, looking down the bar for support.

"Don't know what they expect..." to no one in particular.

I've finished my plate with a Midwesterner's thoroughness, practically licked it clean. I pay, thank the waitress, get up unsteadily, still at sea, and start towards the door. As I pass by the bar a parting splash of indignation.

"Who in hell does she think she is, wagging her butt in my Gary's face?"

The night is warming up.

It is still hot outside, but not as bad as before. I stand on the stoop long enough to let my eyes adjust. A critter is howling in the darkness beyond the road, alarmed or just tired of being alone. *Careful, old timer,* as I feel my way down the uneven steps and onto the uneven sidewalk.

I stop to gape on the way back to the motel, a sliver of moon in the star-flung sky.

"A billion galaxies," a park ranger told me, "Maybe a billion-billion."

How unlikely my parents' eyes would meet, Barbara's and mine for that matter.

I call Barbara back when I get to the hotel. It is good to hear her voice. I catch up on her day, the kids, the teaching she loves, a long bike ride with a friend through the woods.

"October in Michigan," I pipe in. "Best time of the year."

"How about you, Johnny Bob? How are you doing?"

"Pretty used up tonight, in spite of a spectacular

dinner. So hot out there I took off my jacket for most of the afternoon. The heat seemed more dangerous than the road. I know what we agreed to, but" and she steps in.

"It's okay with me if you shed that jacket, whatever it takes to be safe. But beyond that, how are you doing?"

"In spite of the heat, it's most everything I'd hoped for. There's a whole different kind of beauty out here. Stark and hard and borderless. It wears you out and opens you up at the same time. I don't really understand it, but I can feel it happening."

I pause for a moment, but Barbara says nothing.

"A big part of why I'm out here, I think. To check out what remains when all the razzmatazz burns away."

Her turn for a long pause, then "I love that about you, John. What Eric Bibb called 'trusting your cape'."

"Doesn't ring a bell."

"Really? An old song. A good one. It always reminds me of you."

"I'm drawing a blank."

"Eric Bibb. Two b's. Something like 'Trust Your Cape'. Google it when we get off the phone. You'll like it. You are it."

I google Eric Bibb when we hang up, and listen to his rendition of "The Cape." Then listen again, tears now.

"Reminds me of you" may be the second nicest thing Barbara's ever said to me.

CHAPTER 12

TOILETS START FLUSHING before first light, doors slamming, showers running and sinks. A pickup growls awake in the parking lot, radio up high, then surges out onto the road. In spite of my resolve to get an early start, I dawdle over breakfast and a dated USA Today. By the time I mount up, the sun is already at it, hot but not smoldering like yesterday. Not yet, I tell myself, pulling on my jacket.

The jacket comes off within an hour, a heated procession through desert flats dotted with scrub brush and cactus. Driveways festooned with elaborate entranceways funnel out into barbwired emptiness. An occasional cow or two scrounges for something green or munches away at a corrugated hay stand. The road itself is mostly deserted, tattooed with tar patches that go soft in the midday sun. The gouges left by breakaway trailers are deep enough to demand attention, and set the bike awiggle when I don't. Wiggles are not what I'm looking for at any speed, contractions in my hands and forearms that take a half hour to release. The driveway cattle guards keep livestock off the road, a protection not afforded the flattened snakes, scorpions, frogs and lizards in their slippery crematorial repose.

Beyond an unmarked railroad crossing, I pass a blur of power poles and garbage bags, flat roofed garages, sheds, a car off the side of the road, burned out and beginning to rust. I push through a gust out of nowhere, dust, dust, and emerge coughing and spitting, pass a huddle of buildings stripped of their stucco, and beyond them a gas sign with its promise of relief.

I am toasted.

I pull into the station and stagger inside.

The woman behind the counter nods, and keeps talking, phone up under a wad of hair.

"You gotta get yourself some protein, Daddy — ham, grits, eggs. Protein. I'll bring something by as soon as I get off work." She stops as someone is shouting back, then "I'm comin over whether you like it or not."

She looks at me, rolls her eyes and listens.

"You're not hearing, Daddy," and another long pause, hand over the phone, mouthing *yes I am* up at the ceiling.

"Larry and the kid can do just fine without me for a change," another eye-rolled hesitation as I walk back to the cooler, an emphatic "I'll see you about five."

I open the cooler to an exasperated "Men!" I remove

a large bottle of water and a carton of cottage cheese. I pour a cup of lukewarm coffee, add cream and take an acidy sip. When I get up to the counter to pay, she shakes her head and grins.

"You get all that?"

I sit down at a table across from the counter, and get after the cottage cheese with a plastic spoon. She looks over, clearly amused.

"I'm not so sure about the protein in grits."

"Either way," I smile, "Dad's a pretty lucky guy."

I'm feeling refreshed by the time I get back to the cycle, hydrated and caffeinated and lathered with sunblock. I roll into the suburbs of Lubbock an hour later, planning to hunt down the bookstores around Texas Tech. Put off by the sprawl and the traffic, I swing impulsively onto a road that bypasses the city to the south. A breeze is rising in the west, grabbing the whirled attention of wind generators out on the plains. The still-sunny weather is cooling enough that I pull off at an exit and climb back into my jacket.

The road begins a long swing to the north. Perhaps I'll keep going, up into New Mexico by night. The road clears, and my mind with it, as Lubbock recedes in my rearview mirror. These wavy undulations feel like sailing out of a harbor into the open sea. I soon have unencumbered sight lines out to the horizon, and with the miles a gradual erosion of my familiar sense of separateness. Is it possible this small self is a case of mistaken identity?

Out beyond the irrigated cotton fields, the country is getting thirsty. Scattered trees give way to wheat grass and mesquite, an occasional huddle of cattle around well-pumped water and truck-delivered hay. Towns thin out, and in the stretches between them I can go a long time without seeing a car in either direction.

I stop in an empty intersection to wipe off the visor on my helmet. I can't remember the last road sign I've seen. Or car. Or person. In every direction a plain strewn with prickly and distorted looking plants, hugging the dry ground in search of water.

An hour further I come over a rise onto a plain that runs for miles out to a dim outline of hills. The kind of place that gives you room to think expansively or not at all. I pull over, park, and get out of my helmet and jacket. I look in every direction, nothing to obstruct or distract, an openness as nourishing as empty.

I walk up the shoulder and sit down on a pile of gravel by the side of the road. I wiggle down into it and lie back, a cloudless sky above. My thinking slows, then gives way altogether. Only awareness now, a comfortable immersion in everything around me.

At some point a tanker truck rumbles out of the distance and slows to a stop beside me.

"You all right down there?"

"Yes, I am."

After a pause, "You sure?"

"Yup. Just resting. Thanks for stopping to ask."

He says nothing for a moment, just looks.

"Thank you, really. I've never felt better."

I am back out into empty now, refreshed and wide-eyed, down long straightaways under a cathedral sky, and wide, sweeping curves. Small boat on a boundless sea, and for intervals, sea itself.

Time comes to get me as the sun goes orange in the west, first thoughts about where I am and where I'll stay tonight. The stop sign at the first intersection in a long time is a Rorschach card of bullet holes. Outlaws I'm sure and no-goods, more likely drunken teenage boys on an aimless midnight run. There's a small sign next to it, patriot blue and red, a highway to the right. I turn and head North. The sun is on my left for an easy hour, a dust cloud on the horizon. I hear the long sad wail of a train whistle at dusk.

I slow when I come up on a weather-worn sign announcing an expressway entrance. Further on the roar of a passing diesel, a restaurant, the shadowy outline of a town. I pull up to a hamburger joint and park, then rush down between booths of teenagers to the restroom. They seem more interested in their phones than faces. Only one of them looks up to smile at my urgency.

I return from the restroom as casually as possible, glancing at my Fitbit for the time. It is almost 7:00 pm, 9:00 pm back in Michigan. I go out into the parking lot to call Barbara. We have a long conversation about her day, the latest faculty drama at the university where she teaches, a walk on the beach, the kids. I give her a thin review of my day. She wants more.

"So how are you doing?"

"I'm loving it out here." Where are the words? "These wide-open places take a can opener to your tight and tidy sense of self. It reminds me of being at sea for a long haul, how the ocean undermines your sense of separateness, like a wave discovering it is also ocean."

"You okay with that?"

"Yeah, I am. What I wanted really, the connection with everyone and everything that becomes more obvious when I slow down and shut up." Too many words.

When she says nothing, "I'm good. Really. Better than good."

Another long pause.

"I'm still me, tired, dusty, hungry, horny, missing you. Same old crazy, but with the doors and windows open."

Barbara is chuckling now, "Wide open from the sound of it."

I'm more hungry than curious about this silhouette town. In less than a block I turn in under a flashing pizza sign and park.

The sign inside says "Seat yourself." I find a table under a light in the corner, away from a herd of raucous teenagers, shouting and flirting and showing off, food an excuse for hanging out. I thoroughly enjoy a pizza and beer, the buzz and hum of the place.

I take a chilly swing through the town after dinner, and sign in at a plain but clean motel. I pile the gear off my bike onto a spare bed, to sort out in the morning. I pull on a jacket and go outside, walk for a while under a cloudless sky.

I like what happened out there today, raw awareness without all the extras.

I recall the story of a highfalutin' professor of Asian studies who went to a monastery during his sabbatical year to try on what he had been lecturing about for decades. He was met at the door by the spiritual director who bowed solemnly and smiled, then led him to the tearoom. No words were spoken, only a gestured invitation to sit across from each other at a low table. The little monk bowed again, then began to pour tea into the professor's saucered cup. Slowly, very slowly, up to the rim of the cup and kept pouring, running down the side of the cup and into the saucer now, filling it and pouring still, until the startled professor begged him to stop.

"What are you doing?"

Only then did the monk look up, smile and speak.

"The first and most important lesson is that the cup is of value precisely to the extent it is empty."

Empty. What happened out there this afternoon. Awareness only, simple, direct.

I take the long way back, down a tired street past a motel with cabins the shape of tepees. I come across a desolate little parking lot carnival, almost empty at closing time. A few stalls are still open, shelves of stuffed animals, tanks for blowing up helium balloons. Lots of cotton candy and Mountain Dew. There's a pony circle without any ponies and a miniature Ferris wheel that does not inspire confidence. It's the kind of place I dreamed about as a kid.

Several blocks later a freight train rumbles into view, hissing and moaning as it slows to pass, then disappearing out into the flatland black.

I am thoroughly chilled by the time I get back to the motel. A hot shower helps. I slip into a death-deep sleep under a scratchy blanket on a hollowed-out mattress.

CHAPTER 13

OVERRIDING my high-minded reasons not to, I stop at the hamburger place for breakfast in the morning. I feast on an egg and cheese biscuit, and a large coffee with cream. I scan a local newspaper someone's left behind, putting it aside when I realize it is two weeks old. I am hungry for the nourishment of a local bookstore, all the better if they serve up coffee and day-old pastries. Maybe tonight, after the sensory overload of a long day's ride.

I power up the ramp into a nerve-wracking game of hide and seek with a chain of semis headed west. It feels like the batter's box in a diesel-fumed ninth inning, one strike from being out. I take a deep breath, not a whiff of transcendence.

Not only are there diesels, but snakery in the extreme. At every rest stop there are warning signs, keep your distance from "poisonous snakes and insects," two of my favorites. Back on the highway I pass billboard after billboard hawking a tourist trap extravaganza, a clearing house for all things snake. Visions of gaping jaws and Dairy Queen tails make it easy to drive on by.

I break into a long open stretch between the caravans of semis, miles of truckless straightaway out ahead. I gradually come up alongside a freight train heading west. An undeclared cross-country race ensues, Honda and Iron Horse for a sweet ten miles. The Honda blasts through the finish line first but concedes when time-adjusted for weight.

What fun to be sixteen again.

I make a pit stop in the early afternoon. There's a clutter of Gatorade bottles at the end of the exit ramp, filled to varying degrees with what looks like urine. I pull into a gas station and leave my bike at the otherwise empty pump. I wander around the equally empty station, stretching and yawning and killing time. The wide-browed Native American behind the counter watches me wearily. What must local people feel when affluent-looking outsiders roll in with their shiny cars and motor-cycles, carefree about everything but gas and a restroom? I get a carton of milk out of the cooler and a mega cup of Diet Coke.

"How ya' doing?" at the counter gets me a sullen nod.

I stand in the sunshine outside and gulp down the milk. I chase it with Diet Coke out at the pump. Dependency breeds resentment in healthy people. If I'd grown up on an Indian reservation, I'd be sullen too.

I've had enough expressway. I turn down a hardscrabble road and discover that I'm on what's left of Old Route 66. The boom towns of an earlier era are ghost towns now, caved in and abandoned, desiccated hulks strewn alongside the freeways that killed them. Only the rusting highway signs remind you of earlier prominence. There's not much left but history.

When I can take no more, I head north on a road that winds up and down and up again through sun glazed fields dotted with pinyon pine. Townlets come and go with their artisan booths and multi-colored mailboxes, latter-day cowboys with wide brimmed hats and florid bandanas, past bars and grocery stores, porch sitters and rake handlers and dogs wearing fancy collars. I nod acknowledgment as I pass, then it's up and around again, past children bouncing on a trampoline in back of a tin-roofed house.

The money begins to show when I close in on Santa Fe. Glass fronted estates cling to the hillside, solar-powered and shrub-perfect in the late afternoon sun. Women in their yoga gear walk well-groomed pooches on sidewalks so new I can smell the fresh concrete. Up over a ridge now and abruptly down through an unmarked curve circling a small park, hard right into its gravel parking lot, up to what looks like a public restroom.

I walk around afterward, stopping to stretch the ache out of my shoulders and neck. A round-shouldered old man is sitting under a shade tree along the path. Loose jawed and stooped, he is staring down at his fingers, splayed flat on a picnic table. When I try to engage him, "nice evening" and all, he looks at me blankly, pursed lips and a nod, then back down at his hands. He says nothing, does not look up again. I buy us time by stretching for a few minutes, which seems to bother him more than invite.

Sometimes a guy just needs to be alone.

I can't help myself. I wish him a "good evening" before walking back to the parking lot. He does not look up.

The sky is salmon colored out over the hills. It's time to find a place to bunk, that bowl of chili I've been thinking about since noon.

I pull on my helmet and climb back on my bike. Darkness is taking over the park. He is still sitting there. I want to help, but I don't know how. Does love matter?

I twist the key in the ignition.

The Santa Fe I steer into bears no resemblance to the sleepy one I cycled through forty-five years ago. The signs to the famous town plaza lead me into a network of crowded arteries, stops and surging starts, past strip malls and businesses wrapped in counterfeit adobe. Horn-honking SUVs swerve in and out for dinnertime advantage, four-wheeled pandemonium.

I escape into the driveway of the first motel I come to. I am on commotion overload, almost a flashback to deplaning in the bustling Miami Airport after weeks in the jungles of Nicaragua on a Witness for Peace mission. More stimulation than I can take. I walk out beyond the motel to the pool and study the unfazed surface of the water. I lie down on a lawn chair and take a deep breath. Another. First relief from the swirl of noise and movement.

I have rushed by too much of my life.

It's time to step out of the race.

The hotel is more expensive than my regular fare, but I'm not going back out there to shop. When the clerk tells me tomorrow night is filling up, I ask him to reserve a second. I swipe and sign and lug my gear up to a comfortable second-floor room. Let go and enjoy. I've got two nights and a day in this art-glutted town, tucked up in the mountains of a beautiful state. All this and the warm weariness that catches up at the end of a twisting road.

I don't sit at a bar often, so it is fun to climb onto a barstool a half hour later and order a Margarita. I'll head down to the plaza when the traffic clears.

The guy on the barstool next to me is talking to a woman in a confessional tone.

"My life is becoming a series of late afternoon lunches. Thin talk and martinis. Pretty pathetic, huh?"

I try not to listen in on her supportive disclaimers. It's hard not to admire his open admission, perhaps a place to start.

I relax down into the tart Margarita, at peace until I start fumbling through pockets for the key I've left in the Honda's ignition.

I return to the room after retrieving the key. I run a hot washcloth over my face and press hard at the dust in the corners of my eyes. The skin no longer springs back into place but piles up like breakers in a seaside photo. I smile at my enduring vanity, enough time in the bright lights to get cancer of the ego.

Using a map they gave me at the desk, I search out the local bookstore. It is closed for the night. Just as well, I reckon. I might not have pried myself away in time for dinner.

The plaza is quiet, couples mostly, strolling off

dinner under the festooned trees in the square. I am concerned enough about kitchens closing that I settle for the second restaurant I sample. The place is still full, after-dinner warmth competing with the chill creeping through the open doors out onto the square. I ask for a table near the kitchen for warmth. I drape my dayglo jacket over the back of the chair, embarrassed by the pleasure I take from other guests' attention.

"Riding?" the well-groomed waiter asks, leaning in with "good for you" assurance before over-promoting tonight's special. I go along with him in spite of reservations about the price of fish flown in from the coast.

A blue suited business sort is scuffling with himself at the bar, stumbling off his stool onto his cowboy boots, pulling at his nose and coughing, looking wildly around the room. He pulls at his nose again, harder now, and reddens when he catches the bartender staring. He slaps his billfold on the bar to signal for his bill. The room quiets as he waits to pay and escape. People with eyes averted whisper to each other behind palms raised to cover their mouths. He settles up and makes his unsteady way out the door.

I wait too long before following him to the street to make sure he is okay. I look both ways when I get out front. He is nowhere in sight.

The place is quiet when I return to my table,

genuine concern in many people's eyes. I am chagrined at my slow response to his distress, too distracted by the commotion to see the man within.

The restaurant returns to normal in time, cakes and puddings now, spoon-clicking coffees and creams. I work my way through a full plated dinner. The lush salad and over buttered potato forgive the pale flounder. And with honeyed cheese biscuits, renewed admiration for anyone who can push away a half-finished plate. "Enough" was a language unspoken at my father's table, where, as Jim Harrison put it, overeating was considered a form of heroism.

The plaza is almost empty when I walk into the square and snap pictures of the lights strung through the branches of the trees. The pictures do not do justice to the beauty, like words falling short of experience. I tuck the phone away and gape. For a few moments thinking surrenders altogether, a little boy's amazement and awe.

My pace slows on the way back to the parking lot. I am haunted by the image of a woman several tables away at the restaurant, unnoticed until deep into my meal. She sat stoically at her table across from an empty chair and a second half empty glass of wine. She sipped from her glass, almost caressing it between sips. And waited. A solicitous waiter stopped by occasionally, leaning down I suspect to ask her if she wanted anything else. Tears filled her eyes when whomever she came with did not return.

How to accept what I cannot fix?

I get so chilled on the ride back to the motel that my shuddering makes it difficult to steer. I veer off into the parking lot of a strip mall and jump off, slapping my hands together, then against my chest, to get the blood circulating. I stomp my boots on the asphalt, then pace back and forth in front of a string of small shops. A light is on in one of them, a "closed" sign pulsing in the window. On my second pass, I stop and glance in. Two men in soiled aprons are seated on either side of a chopping block covered with a towel. They are shouting and laughing, gesturing wildly. It takes a moment to realize they are playing checkers.

CHAPTER 14

I AM BACK AT "COLLECTED WORKS" bookstore when they open in the morning. My stomach is a bit queasy. I took no breakfast to offset the handful of medication I washed down before climbing on my bike. Fortunately, they have a coffee bar and a good selection of yogurts. I settle at a table with a wide view of the street.

A procession of people file by on the sidewalk outside. Tourists mostly, bright eyed and ruddy, hand-holding retirees in chattering knots, tour buses rumbling at the end of the street. In among the others an occasional road weary young family, baby-carriaged fathers, patient as plow horses, and mothers weighed down with baby gear and domestication, fixed expressions and wedding bands, eyes hardening at the giddy spontaneity and too-available cleavage of their youngers. Even in picturesque Santa Fe, being a human is hard work. A gift sure enough, but also back-breaking and at least occasionally, spirit-testing.

I stay too long among the books, walking out after noon with a single purchase.

I wander streets brimming with art and Native American artifacts. There aren't many weatherworn blue jeans in this part of town. Shops full of silver and turquoise jewelry, necklaces, earrings, tendered by saleswomen with honeyed complexions, working hard and required to look their best. Not so the chalky faced teenager who scurries out of the backroom with a clutch of shoeboxes and beaded handbags.

I can only guess what any of them thinks or feels, the weight of detail or circumstance.

I don't need particulars to admire them.

———

I get drowsy soon after a street counter lunch. I walk up to the square, kick off my boots, sprawl in the grass and drift off to sleep. When a church bell wakens me with its late afternoon toll, I sit up and look around. Several ragged looking men have joined me, strewn on the grass or hunched over rolled up sleeping bags on nearby benches. The shopping crowd has thinned on the sidewalk beyond.

I do not want the day to slip away. I pull on my boots and lace them, then head in the direction of the bells, a distinct memory of a nearby cathedral. I find the two-spired Basilica of Francis of Assisi a block from the square and walk up the steps through the front door. The pillars take my eyes up to the high arches they support, and above them the great expanse within the canopy. Evening mass is underway, priest and congregation a distant miniature from the back of the church.

I walk to a side chapel and sit down on a hard wooden bench. The sound of the Mass has almost disappeared, swallowed up by the immensity around it. I drift into a stillness that feels like home, empty and wide awake.

I stroll the terracotta floors of the La Fonda Hotel an hour later, the adobe and beam elegance of the place. I find my way to the restaurant, the rush of memory it evokes.

I am on my first cross country run, late June of 1971. After a night of carrying on in Taos, I wake up next to a hot spring pool on a bluff above the road out of town. There are a few tents and vans scattered around, but no one who is stirring. I wiggle around in my damp sleeping bag, looking for relief for a stiffened shoulder. I fall back to sleep. When I wake at dawn the sky has gone orange. A cool breeze rustles the scrub brush around me. I prop myself up to look around. And there she is, sitting comfortably on the edge of the pool across from me, feet and calves dangling down in the water. She is naked.

"Hello" she says, a lilt in her voice, a smile at my surprise.

"Good morning," nothing suave about it, a spectacular way to begin a day. While I am wrestling out of my tangled sleeping bag, she lowers herself into the steaming water and breaststrokes slowly down the length of the pool.

I pull on my dew-soaked jeans and boots, stagger off to the bushes to pee. When I return she is gone, I suspect to a bumper-stickered van across the pool. *Did that just happen?* I know it did, her water-splashed exit glistens on the side of the pool.

In the early afternoon I cycle down a rutted clay path onto the road to Santa Fe. Within a few miles I am joined by a fellow rider who motors up from behind. He pulls alongside me and nods, granny glasses, Fu Manchu mustache, hair flailing back, a regular transplant from Easy Rider. We ride side by side for the rest of the afternoon, at one point getting blown onto the sandy shoulder of the road by a gust screaming out of a gouge in the wall of rock.

We pull into a gas station on the outskirts of Santa Fe and compare notes over the gas pump. His name is Bill. Like me, he's out for an extended ride.

"You know this town?"

"Never been here."

"Lots to do here," he says. "I'm heading down to

Albuquerque tonight, but let me show you around." He leads me over to the town square to have a beer before he takes off.

Within an hour, we are sitting in the restaurant at the La Fonda hotel. We're only a swig or two into our beers when Bill nudges me and whispers.

"Don't look now, but Lee fricking Marvin just walked in. Heard he was down here to do a movie. He's right behind you."

I shift my chair in the direction Bill's looking, enough that I can see who he's talking about. A very red-faced Lee Marvin is standing a few tables away, an attractive middle-aged woman in tow. Hands on his hips, he is surveying the almost empty room. He squints when he gets to us, then lurches straight for our table. He pulls up abruptly in front of Bill, swaying back and forth, looking him over and scowling. He skips the introductions.

"What do we have here?" back over his shoulder to his startled companion. "Looks like a real live hippy."

Bill is trying to keep his cool. He says nothing.

"Probably one of those anti-war protestors," he seethes, leaning over Bill, swiping spittle off his lips with the back of his hand.

"He's not," I blurt, earning me a glare. "But I am."

He lunges over the table, growling, grabbing my shirt with one large paw, almost knocking the table over when he yanks me off my chair.

"Please, Lee, stop!" His girlfriend is on him from

behind, swinging around in front of him when he turns, palms up high on his chest.

"Please, Honey. Stop."

It takes a moment for it to register, and then his face sags. Without looking at Bill or me, he lets go, dropping me back onto my chair. He stares at her for a long moment, then takes her hand and lumbers toward the door.

The skirmish is over, but not the war.

That was then and this is now. Tonight's band is assembling a wide array of instruments off in the corner. Dinner guests are lining up at the hostess stand for seating. I am getting hungry, and without much thought get in line.

When my turn comes, I ask for a small table under a light and order a Margarita. I take out the book I purchased earlier, then put it back in the bag without opening it. Nothing wrong with being alone.

The room seems smaller than it did forty-five years ago, like re-visiting the neighborhood where you grew up, a miniature of the one lived in at seven. The restaurant is filling up rapidly with an affluent looking crowd. Rather than feeling out of place, I am comfortable with my relative vagrancy. The uniform of privilege has always seemed a little silly. That I am also privileged seems both unlikely and undeserved, a gift that allows me the luxury of this road trip, the meal I order and the drink beside it. That I have come up short on many occasions is a gift also, failure a better teacher than success. Gratitude seems the only sane response, gratitude and how to put privilege to work. Isn't *paying forward* really *paying back?*

It is no surprise that the table next to me is the last to be taken. A middle-aged man with a perfectly manicured beard pulls up a chair and sits. His shapely companion composes herself on the pew-like bench we share. I can only see her out of the corner of my eye, which is more than enough.

The music begins in the course of our meals, so rhythmic and original it defies genre. Knives and forks are set down on plates all around us. Women shift in their seats, then the subtlest of sways, trying not to embarrass their more subdued companions. The woman next to me crosses and uncrosses her legs while attempting to maintain conversation. Her gilded sandal dangles out beside me from the toe of her perfect foot.

I walk by the basilica on my way back to the plaza. Beneath the trees in the square with their bedazzling white lights, there's a lingering odor of fresh human feces.

I am uncomfortable with the vague smugness I felt among my gussied-up companions at the restaurant. As if money, not our relationship to it, is what matters most. I am clearly not as smart or secure as I'd like to think, or as generous as I could be. It is well past time to trade judgment for understanding and do what I can without taking account. *Paying forward* is more than a slogan.

Armed with high-mindedness, I catch myself trying to avoid eye contact with a man whose dog I stop to pet. We talk for a few minutes. More accurately, he talks, a seething barrage about the state of the world and eventually his dog's need for some "*real* dog food."

I crouch down to scratch behind his sidekick's ears — "He sure seems like a good guy" — then back up to make a contribution.

"I've got to get on my way," at some point during his almost seamless progression of tangled associations. "It's been good talking to you."

We shake hands and I walk on, the ease of romanticizing solitude or life close to the bone. It's one thing to choose to live frugally or alone, quite another to have either imposed on you.

CHAPTER 15

I CATCH up with Barbara before going down to breakfast. After her review of all things Michigan, I launch into a verbal tour of Santa Fe.

"I can't wait to come back here with you."

"Just eight months of teaching," she assures, "then we'll hit the road again."

I make myself at home at the fancy breakfast bar. Rather than memorize the morning paper, I memorize a bowl of fresh raspberries, one at a time. An old couple is sitting side by side at a nearby table. They sway back and forth, in and out of unison, always stopping in a lean towards each other. She seems to be doing most of the talking, mouth up next to his ear as if sharing a secret. He nods and smiles at everything she says. Then it's back to swaying. They stop every now and then to empty coffee-filled saucers back into their cups, heads wagging and mumbling when they dribble on the table-cloth. I wish Barbara were here to smile at our future.

I stop fastening gear to my cycle long enough to shake a cramp out of my fingers. I look up just as a hot air balloon glides out over a ridge a short distance away. A few minutes later there's another, the thrust of a heater in the gondola beneath it. I mention my sightings to the desk clerk when I cash out.

"They're everywhere down here," he explains. "We have weekend rallies where hundreds of them show up, and a zillion tourists to see them. Can't get a motel room for miles around."

Back in the parking lot I see a cluster of balloons off to the southeast. I'm suddenly back in the Azore Islands, sharing a glass of wine with a fellow sailor in the cockpit of our boat. Out of nowhere he tells me of a balloon ride he and his siblings purchased for their aging father's birthday, a surprise his father had always wanted, but only rarely mentioned. He recounts his father's delight when taking off with our friend's sister and a crew, and the horror a short time later when an unanticipated gust drove them into a Texas powerline — the explosion and fire, cascading in flames into a bramble patch below, their charred remains unreachable until a chainsaw crew arrived.

It is not the picture I wanted to take into a long day's ride.

I work my way down narrow streets through a neighborhood of small adobe houses, pastel window frames and doorways, cars up on blocks, backyards with swing sets and picnic tables. I burst onto a service road alongside a northbound expressway, an hour of easy, then onto a more interesting two-laner into the mountains.

Interesting becomes challenging when I enter a river-formed canyon. The road narrows as it climbs, a series of loops and hairpins now, rock walls on one side, river on the other. I lurch through curve after cross-festooned curve, each with its own story of lost control and death. I breathe my way through engine howling downshifts, slowing as I go. My forearms tighten, wringing smoothness out of the back and forth. I have little traffic to contend with until I round a blind curve and swerve to avoid a dump truck that strays over the centerline. How many accidents leave half-eaten sandwiches on the floor of the cab?

I pull over to stretch and relax. The thin margin between the cliff face and road does not allow much time for either. I carve my way through a tense half hour before the canyon opens out into warm afternoon sunlight, pinyon pine and juniper now, the soothing smell of fir. Confidence is seeping back into me when I come up over a rise, then dip suddenly down toward the fresh carcass of a shiny brown horse. Two white pickups have stopped on the other side of the road where a man in overalls is unspooling a steel towline from the winch mounted on his truck.

I slow almost to a stop and swing around the animal as a truck comes barreling up from behind. I cannot entirely avoid the splash of blood on the road, my rear tire wiggling for traction as I pass. I hope the last gallop was a good one, time in the bright sun outside the corral.

Signs to Taos begin to appear, in differing arrays of pastel enthusiasm. None of them mentions the ranch D.H. Lawrence made famous when struggling with tuberculosis during his later years.

I could use some gas and something wet. I pull into a station on the outskirts of town, fill the tank and scrub road debris off my visor. On the way into the station I pass by a Native American woman sitting on a lawn chair in the sun. A baby strapped into a stroller beside her is squealing excitement at anyone who passes by. When I stop to smile at her and make faces, she responds with tears and a bellow. I apologize to her mother, who forgives me with a crooked smile.

I make a stop at the restroom, pick up milk and water, pay and walk out into the sunshine. Mother and baby have moved on. I settle into the lawn chair and uncap the milk. A gaggle of grade school girls huddle nearby, waiting for a classmate to come out of the store. They are giggling about "titties" with excited anticipation, clasping their hands over their mouths in sham embarrassment. They cover their eyes only to peek out at each other and explode in laughter. I want to thank them for temporary relief from the too vivid image of the horse hurtling to death.

I flinch at the snarl of a dirt bike across the road, the chatter of its over-throttled engine. I am amazed it doesn't fly apart, revved above the redline and revved again. The bike bursts out from behind a garage with a metallic scream, front tire in the air, pencil thin teenager just hanging on.

I go back into the gas station and ask the woman behind the counter about the hot spring pool I remember.

"I've heard of it," running her fingers up into her hair, "but I'm not sure where it is. I just moved out here six months back," open palms out beside her. "Sorry."

The past is never really past. The best parts and worst travel with us. If not in our conscious minds, in the memory of cells. I spend the next hour crisscrossing Taos in search of a long dormant memory.

It is 1971 again. After eight years of monastery

training and six more earning a doctorate, I am actively exploring life outside the lines, always spontaneous, sometimes messy, at least occasionally a disaster.

I cycle down from Colorado to Taos on Friday afternoon and pull in at a restaurant with some motorcycles out front. It is dark when some Native Americans I have eaten with offer to give me a tour of the town. I climb into the back of a pickup with two of them. Our driver and his girlfriend lead us on a directionally challenged tour of every lumpy road in Taos. At some point we pile out for a totally unneeded second round of drinks. We can stop here, and we should. We don't.

I don't remember much of the ride after that, only truck headlights veering off the road, across a yard and up onto a white brick wall. We carom off the back of the cab. The engine roars and roars again during unsuccessful attempts to back the truck off the rubble. Lights are coming on in houses around us, threats and a lot of yelling. We pile out of the truck, and run between houses and down deserted streets, splitting up as we go. I stagger back to my bike before dawn.

Sometimes we eat our distress, sometimes drink or smoke it. When you are young and dumb, you don't feel the need to choose between them. You might end up vomiting afterwards, which is what I did in the parking lot before following the sunrise out into the hills.

I am not looking for drama today. A walk-around would be good, a hot plate and a cold beer, a warm bed in a clean room. I park my bike in the town square and set out on foot.

If Taos is the energy vortex that legend suggests, it is becoming a conflicted and pricey one. Shops full of fine Southwestern artistry share the streets with temples to tourist consumption. Buy a decaled something or other to remind yourself that you were here, or assure others when you get back home. The sort of places we lived for on the two-week family vacations Dad and Mom wedged into my father's demanding schedule.

No sense in getting high and mighty about it now. There are a lot of kids in the back seats of those SUVs, shouting excitement at their weary parents.

I am surprised to discover a miniature La Fonda hotel back in the square. I step aside at the entryway for a mustached Buddha in a black t-shirt, bald and bright eyed as he bounces by on the balls of his slippered feet.

"That ship has sailed," to no one in particular.

"Sailed!" in case anyone hasn't heard.

The desk clerk answers my questions about D.H. Lawrence with something less than enthusiasm. He does tell me that the hotel has a room with several original Lawrence paintings. When I light up, he assures me that it is temporarily closed.

"Any idea when it will reopen?" gets me a very somber "Not sure about that."

He nods at my dayglo jacket as I am leaving and tells me Lawrence was killed in a motorcycle accident.

"His wife bought it for him, a birthday present," he adds, just the hint of a smile.

I stop in the street outside, wondering if he was only messing with me.

Author, painter and motorcycle enthusiast? The boy had range. The English had a mythical fascination with the desert, Lawrence of Arabia and all. D.H. Lawrence returned over and over to the sand and stone of New Mexico. Aberrations, or an almost predictable response to claustrophobic England?

And what of my love of wide open places, the ocean and more lately the Southwest? Could that be a symptom of some vague claustrophobia to my narrowing capabilities, the dark tunneled certainty of death?

I can't help but smile at my unlimited capacity for self-absorption. I am reminded of two young aspirants attempting to one-up each other on the respective powers of their spiritual leaders. One gestures at the opposite bank of a river and wags his finger.

"My master is so powerful that he can point at objects across the river and move them." He didn't say "Top that," but could have. His young friend smiles and replies.

"My master is so wise that he eats when he is hungry and goes to sleep when he is tired."

Bereft of anything approaching wisdom, I am more hungry than discriminating. I settle in over a plate of garlic shrimp and beer. When restraint might have me asking for my bill, the waiter reels me in with "dark chocolate drizzled over whatever flavor ice cream you fancy." And when I hesitate, "just scrumptious."

I take a long walk afterwards, as if penance can be done. I come up alongside a yard with a bamboo screen wired to a chain link fence, to screen out I don't know what. People like me perhaps. I try unsuccessfully to calm a wisp of a dog barking outrage up and down the fence line. He almost decapitates himself on the seat of a plastic chair before stumbling into a minefield of beer cans. The racket sets off a baby's wailing somewhere within the stucco square of the house.

I walk on briskly, animal whisperer in full retreat. Calmer now, a block beyond commotion, I emerge from under a line of trees into a full conspiracy of clouds and sunset, low mountain profiles like great slumbering animals, going blue over time under an incomplete moon. Beauty for only looking up.

CHAPTER 16

I TOUCH base with Barbara in the morning, get a fresh read on how she and the kids are doing, the latest antics of our no-good dog. A cold September is lighting up the trees around our house. I have more than a twinge of longing for Barbara and home, the sweet tension that builds when we are apart.

"It's kind of foggy out here this morning. I'm not sure what's happening in the mountains."

"It's not the ocean, John. You can take your time to decide."

"I'll get a better reading when the fog clears."

"Just..."

"I know, I'll be safe. I love you too."

I muscle past a stack of free newspapers on the way to the breakfast room. Why is it so hard to do one thing at a time? Is it too late to learn?

I linger over a pile of pancakes and strawberries, a

cup too many of the rich dark coffee. I put my fork down between bites. If I'm going to eat something this good, it's blasphemy not to enjoy it.

A stoop-shouldered old timer is sitting two booths down, eyes brimming with pain. He sighs defeat, then sighs again. His gaze never rises from the formica table-top. I want to ladle out some easy grace, tell him it will be okay.

It may not be okay, may never be okay.

He comes to life when the waitress brings him breakfast, the redemption of french toast and a smile.

I stand in the parking lot and study the sky, well aware that cross country riding, like ocean crossing, answers to Mother Nature.

In the years at sea, Barbara and I learned to tell friends who wanted to visit that they could suggest either where or when they would like to meet.

"We can't promise anything if you want to know both."

The weather is the boss, pure and simple. You listen and adjust or get in trouble. In spite of my instinct to forge ahead, there are worse things than waiting. I know because I have not always waited.

The boss is sending mixed signals this morning. The fog seems to be dissipating, but not going away entirely. The sun is occasionally breaking through the overcast sky. The breeze is mild, but frigid. The weather forecast suggests a mix of sunshine and cloud.

I'm not sure what to do.

I go up to the room and work a lining of thermal underwear under my jeans and jacket. I strap rain gear to the outside of my bag where I can get to it quickly. When I finally climb on the bike, I put gloves aside and pull on a pair of mittens.

I'm chagrined about the mittens, but most of all cold, the price of medicine-thinned blood. I look around, still lots of fog, hopefully enough sun to burn it away.

The first half hour doesn't tell me anything. I motor through town and out onto a cardboard-colored plain, a mountainous horizon out beyond. You like open, I remind myself. This is open. I cross the shining silver Gorge Bridge, a two-lane tightrope over the Rio Grande. I have been here before, but I can't help but stop. I pull into a crowded parking lot and walk back out to a viewing area in the center of the span. I feel a surge of vertigo as I lean out to look down into the gorge. Unstable rock walls disappear six hundred feet below into the rapids of what seems like a miniature river. I try not to think of the bridge's long history as a suicide site.

I look to the horizon to offset the queasiness I feel, a recent and unwelcome addition to my old man woes. *Deal with it, John.* I stride back to the parking lot, trying to summon the animal resolve I do not feel. There are still few clues in the sky, only an occasional glint in the overcast. Those high clouds are moving fast. I do not stop for coffee at the brightly colored food truck in the parking lot. It's time to get a move on.

I pass clusters of uninterested bighorn sheep on a long, slow uphill grade over miles of scrub brush plain. There's a brief tease of warmth during the infrequent breaks in the clouds. The riding is easy enough, but with unsettling glimpses of those racing clouds far above.

I enter an old growth forest, maple and oak in spite of the elevation, and what looks like white pine. Warmth leeches out of me as I climb, long easy curves mostly, each more chilled than the last. Moisture is building up under my visor.

I glide by alpine meadows, over a rise and another, but always ascending. Cool goes cold as the miles go by, up into a cloudy overhang. Nothing is flowering at this altitude, a haze out over what I guess are spectacular views. I pass boulders and bedrock alongside the road, vague outlines of mountains beyond.

A dangerous cold is taking over. I reel into a fogged-over lookout and stop, add a layer of fleece under my jacket. Even with Michigan mittens, my fingers are knotting up. The clock is running. I jump back on my bike and surge out onto the road. I swoop into hollows and up over rises, through dark patches of shade under the pine.

I burst out into the open for flashes of sunlight, past

pull outs where haze blankets overhang views. Then onto a ridgeline for a long, frozen stretch, a first tantalizing downward drop, just in time, a heaviness in my chest. I begin a serpentine descent, downshifting to slow my momentum.

I warm up during an hour of low country cruising through a string of sleepy towns. I resist the urge to stop, buying as many miles as I can.

I finally pull into a cinder-strewn driveway in front of a gas station with a single pump. There are swirls of color in the puddles around me, a mixture of water and gas. I sit for a while before climbing off, stumble when I catch my heel on the seat.

I dig out a credit card and am filling the tank when the station door slams open behind me. A red-faced man strides towards me, his wispy white hair a halo over his shoulders. I exhale when he stomps by, his mane fairly crackling with electricity. His sidekick hurries to catch up, a whiff of mothballs when he shuffles by. Angel Hair yanks his truck door open, steps up on the running board, and shouts at his companion over the cab.

"Just for the record, I don't need any more of that shit."

Two doors slam, then an over-revved ignition and a cinder-laden cloud of high-ho-Silver.

A bellyful of chili and I'm back on the road. The riding is easy through a series of long, scenic valleys, Native American reservations on either side of the road. I pass a disquieting number of roadside crosses, clusters of two or three sometimes, often where graveled driveways spill out onto the road. Mobile homes in varying states of disrepair try to blend into the mountains behind them. I don't want to think what we've done to the people who live here.

It's getting warm now, even under the sunless sky. I pull up into a party store parking lot to peel off a layer of fleece. I lean down to talk with a raggedy old dog sprawled under the truck beside me. His tail drums against the almost empty gas tank above him.

A gigantic Native American stands behind the counter, proud eyes, broad brow, the muscular language of a broken nose. He is kindly enough but reserved, responding to questions about the road ahead with "high" and "beautiful." He leans over to the window and cranes his neck to look up at the sky. He straightens up, looks at me, nods toward the window without saying more.

I take his lead and move to the window, strings of cirrus clouds flying above the haze, fleeting glimpses of the sun. I'm still not sure about this weather. I move back to the counter to pay for my coffee. He takes my cash with an open hand, calloused palm and the stumps of several severed fingers.

Down country warmth fades fast when I start climbing. Green turns brown in pastures bordered by juniper and beech. The temperature drops with every degree of incline. The fog returns and thickens, giving me only brief glimpses of what's coming. In one break I see an ominous smudge up on the summit.

I am driving in a light mist now, what looks like a shadow of rain up ahead. There's no good place to pull off in the narrowing trough, the road angling up into deepening shadows and suddenly available overhangs. Where's an overpass when I need it?

I accelerate when raindrops begin to splatter on my visor, looking for a sheltered place to pull off. Finding none on an upgrade run of switchbacks, I swing off abruptly into some already mushy gravel on the shoulder. I bound off the bike and out of my cycling jacket, pulling on another layer of fleece, then my jacket and foul weather gear. I trade mittens for a pair of thick wool gloves that hold some heat even when wet. They are soaked by the time I climb back on the bike.

"This is your time, Honda."

I power out of the sludge and onto the road. I feel my way up through switchback after switchback, slowing as I go because of the greasy feel of the road.

Instead of washing out, the fog is getting thicker, shrinking my line of sight. Fortunately I seem to be alone out here, no traffic to contend with. I open my face shield enough to lessen the buildup of fog inside the visor.

I grip down hard as I break out of the switchbacks and directly into the storm. I am shocked by the sheer velocity of the wind — squall winds if I were out in the ocean, gusting hard enough to blow me off the road. I bank into them when they try to take me, flatten out when they give way. I hunch down to reduce their drag, lock my vision to the road.

I am still going uphill on a bald ridgeline, naked out in the windswept open. The rain intensifies, blinding horizontal blasts, then taking a breath before blasting again. I lean into them at their fury worst, back off to avoid swerving in the vacuum behind.

This is not a squall blowing through. The wind is building, gale force now, the first flash of lightning, a deafening crack, and right behind it another. No mercy here, a fight to hold on.

I am soaked through and freezing, beyond trembling to spasm. I shake my elbows to loosen up, but it doesn't help. I am losing any fluidity of movement. I have no place to hide, no idea how far, or how far I am able.

Just stay with it in this gust driven curve, lean and hold, hold, ease off and begin again.

Pandemonium now, a crack so loud I duck my head and when I raise it, a clatter against my visor, first wave of sleet, visible sheets off my neck and helmet, the instinct to brake, trying not to hydroplane or slide on the marble-sheened pavement.

I have nowhere to stop on this sleet-strewn road, and death by exposure if I do. Only go on, slower to maintain some traction, hold on and ride it into another broadside of wind, lean and hold for as long as you can.

The timeless blur of lean and hold is eating away at my will and reserve. Then a sudden dip downward, too cold and exhausted to do anything but hang on, into a wide loop now, off to the left another, then down and down into a weakening wind, a soft roll to the right, already milder, rain suddenly down to a drizzle, a slight left and straighten, a half-mile runway, warming as I go, upshifting into a purring fourth gear, the lights of a truck in the opposite direction, the weight and sting of after-spray, and I don't care, I am alive and gliding and getting warmer, wet and empty and alive.

I motor on for a brain-dead while, unzip my rain gear to let the air in. I roll into a small, sun-warmed town on autopilot. I pass a clapboard church with a sign out front that reads "Be the church," which I find heartening. Less so a pawn shop with what I hope is a playful "Cash or Beer." Without benefit of forethought I pull off the road in front of a place with "Food" up over the door. Nothing more.

I feel pure joy, or something like it when I switch off the engine. Relief from the overfocus the day has demanded. Slow motion in a place that stands still. Time to free range for a while and walk around, maybe even stay for the night. I push the kickstand down, two boots on the ground and lean over, face next to the gas tank.

"You did great up there. Thank you."

I shift my weight and drag a leg over, the uncertainty of standing up straight. I reach up for relief from the ache in my shoulders and windmill my arms around. I stand in place until I'm good and ready. Those first steps are not pretty.

I walk a knotty ache of a circle, kick my boots off and pour them out. I peel off my raingear and jacket and spread them over the bike to dry. I step back into my boots, then it's off down a street with its predictable shops, but an almost eerie absence of people. The joy of walking entirely for pleasure, down one block, across, and back on the other side. Thoughtless, wordless also, except to the brown dog waiting at the corner.

"How you doing, Buddy?" A flurry of wagging, but not a word to say. He leans in as I kneel down to scruffle behind his ear, warm eyes, a saliva-frothed smile. No questions about how I did or why, enough that I'm here and scratching. I grunt back to my feet and move on, the lingering wisdom of doghood.

Back at the bike, I pull off the fleece and pull on a flannel shirt. I re-arrange my wet clothes on the handlebars, hoping they will dry before evening dew settles in. I enter the restaurant's welcome warmth, take a menu from the counter to a table near the bar. The place is as empty as main street. Where is everybody?

An unshaven man in an orange corduroy shirt eventually comes out of the kitchen and over to my table.

"Heard you pull up," an off-center smile. "Come over the pass?"

"Not sure what it was. I couldn't see much. But come over I did."

When he nods, I add, "Scared the bejesus out of me."

"You're not the first, partner." And when I say nothing, "Got more balls than me, that's for sure."

"Balls or brainless?" and we chuckle, old friends now.

"How about I get you a beer?" I order the label he suggests.

"Folks round here like it a lot," he assures.

I go back to the menu when he steps away. My fondness for local cuisine got tested back in Taos, a midnight eruption in my motel bathroom. I steer to the well-rutted center of the menu, cheese enchiladas and the like. I settle on vegetarian lasagna and garlic bread.

"Not likely to be kissing anyone tonight," I tell him.

"Now don't be giving up on yourself," he grins, then heads off to the kitchen.

A few people straggle in, mostly one at a time. Some couples join them during my meal, Saturday night and all. And still more singles, settling on barstools near my table.

I'm getting up to leave when what's left of an old man feels his way through the doorway. He puts one foot carefully in front of the other, and aims for the bar. He says nothing when I ask if I can help, just continues on his chinless way, head out front on a wisp of a neck. He gives me a halfhearted nod as he passes, what's left of a smile, no teeth to speak of, then up onto a barstool with a practiced efficiency.

"There you go," he mutters with understandable satisfaction, and reaches down to rearrange the black-handled revolver holstered to his belt.

I walk back to the bike to gather up my clothes, the old guy stuck in my head. He calls up the awe Barbara and I had for ancient bicycle riders in the Netherlands, vital old women talking and pedaling, walkers strapped to their bikes.

"How do you think we'll be at 80?"

"Just like we are now," Barbara grins, "only with more aches and pains."

It's getting late in Michigan when I reach Barbara. I get a lift just from hearing her voice, her sunny rundown of the day. When she asks about mine, I clutch for a moment, unsure how to tell her without causing alarm. She is the lucid member of our relationship, the solid center around whom I orbit in flames. But she is not fireproof.

"Do you remember how you reminded me I'd be okay before I left on the Atlantic solo?"

"Yes," then hesitation. "And you were."

"The short form is that I'm okay."

"Why don't I find that more reassuring?" When I say nothing, "How about the long form?"

Where to start? "Well, the weather was difficult today."

"How difficult?"

"Very. Foggy most of the day. Cold up in the mountains. Freezing really, and windy."

She waits.

"Lots of rain. And some sleet."

"Sleet?"

"Yeah, sleet too. A real mess."

"Cold rain, and wind, and sleet? Are you okay?"

"I'm okay. Now. It was difficult up there."

"Jeez, John..."

Just tell her. "Actually, it was very difficult. That storm at sea when all you can do is hang on. Beyond hard, dangerous."

"Dangerous?"

"Yeah, dangerous." And when she says nothing, "First time in my life that I felt real terror. Thought I felt it before, but I was wrong. This was terror."

"John," and tapering off.

"I don't ever want to feel that way again."

Silence for a long time.

"Then don't." And after an awkward pause, "Please be safe."

We talk for a long time, an unspoken reluctance to hang up. For my part, a hardened determination not to undermine her generosity and courage, the confidence we have in each other.

I close with a commitment to "be okay."

And, years later, "I know you will."

I check into a dated motel down the street, pile my gear on a bed that promises nothing. Even with a full stomach I am teetering near exhaustion. I am also wide awake. To avoid languishing in the too available mildew, I go for a walk.

Evening is doing her best to distract me. There's magic up in the mountains to the west, a sky going scarlet to purple then black. There's an even more extravagant rampage of colors on the underside of the clouds. Venus emerges in the deepening darkness, evening's consolation when mid-ocean. She will ride alone for half an hour before inviting constellations to join her.

What to do with the avalanche of images reignited during the conversation with Barbara? I stop under a flickering streetlamp and take out a pen, try to pin today's impressions to the notecards I carry in my hip pocket. I scribble single words and phrases mostly, relief from the weight of them, insurance against forgetting.

This could go on all night if I let it. I stuff the cards back in my pocket and walk on.

Nature has a way of putting self-importance in its place — weather forecasters with their brave assuredness, even the most seasoned sailor or cyclist in a great storm on the open expanse.

What do you really control? To reef or not when the sea goes black, change the angle of attack on a wind-ravaged road. You do what you can. It works or it doesn't. You live or are damaged or you die.

And what of that larger life with its unknowns and inevitables? The loss of a beloved spouse or a cherished friend. The worry about children whose struggles you cannot fix. The advancing and intractable illness, the steep decline in energy and hope. The stark inevitability of death.

What do you control beyond how you respond to what you most certainly don't control?

CHAPTER 17

MILDEW or not I sail down into that deeper sea, the sleep of the almost dead. I wake up to find that the sheet beneath me has shifted during the night, exposing a cartography of stains on the mattress beneath.

It doesn't matter on this sunny morning. I climb out of bed without a groan, no ache in my back, neck or shoulder. Swollen fingers and palms, but nothing else.

I luxuriate in a long hot shower, then shave and brush my teeth. The man in the mirror is smiling, and over oatmeal and toast a half hour later, quite happy to be alive.

"Somebody's in a real good mood," when the waitress stops by with a coffee refill.

"Feeling good."

When she asks why, I tell her about yesterday's storm.

"A real beauty," I assure her, "one I didn't see coming."

She squints disbelief and moves on, leaving me to reminisce.

I have fond memories of calm days mid-ocean. What I remember best are a few great storms, the "beauty and terror" Rilke described.

I am no fan of risk or danger. I do enjoy a life of extension, those places where competence and challenge seem evenly matched. I have deep reservations about what some call "the fetishization of thrill." It seems adolescent at best, at worst an addiction, a thinly disguised ego trip or death wish.

Yesterday was a mistake. I let the forecast override what I could see with my eyes. It was a dangerous mistake, one I don't need to make twice.

I tire of running yesterday through a strainer. I ask for my check, pay, and go out into the sunshine. A tiny old woman is standing by my bike with her purse and her white-haired dog. He snarls when I reach down to "good dog" him. I expect her to step away but she doesn't, only tightens the shawl around her head. She has the small eyes of a frightened animal, but strangely unfocused. She is gazing out beyond my bike, whispering both sides of a bewildering conversation.

"Running off with a man that way, nuttin' to say to the one she had."

"Hmm."

"Not a word."

"Go figure."

I try to engage her, nice morning and all, but she seems intent on keeping her own company. I glance up the street in the direction she is looking, a very empty place for all the buildings.

The asphalt feels good beneath me. It is not warm yet but headed in that direction. The high mountain road ahead is supposed to be beautiful. There's not much of that scenery yet, scrawny over-fenced pastures mostly, drooping outbuildings short of a barn. An occasional yard full of children stop what they're doing to stare at the man on the motorcycle. Seventy years beyond my yard-staring days, I wonder what they see. Through my young eyes travel was all adventure, *romance and adventure* I had decided by college.

The thought of another mountain, beautiful or not, gnaws away at my warm-belly sense of wellbeing. Signs announcing elevation are becoming more frequent. I pull into a station that advertises itself as the last place to gas up for a long stretch of miles. I pick my way across the cratered gravel to the gas pumps and study the horizon while topping off. A mixture of sunlight and cloud is spilling over the suddenly available bluffs, light-saturated, almost wispy but rolling. Nothing like the shroud over the peaks yesterday. My shoulders and neck contract, the grip I have on the gas nozzle.

I smiled when I first read Thomas Hobbe's admission that "Fear and I were born twins." Not in derision, although there was some of that. It took a while to appreciate the fears I came by early and honestly. Still later the difference between feeling afraid and living afraid. Fear and I have become friends over the years. I'll listen, but it better come packing a clear-eyed argument. Like yesterday. Fear had the goods, and I didn't take them seriously.

I stop several times on my way into the station, turn and stare and study.

I'll be damned if I'll make the same mistake today.

I pace outside the restroom, then try the door again. A glassy-eyed old gentleman finally emerges with a smiling apology for taking so long.

"No problem," I assure him, then rush to the urinal. The door rattles behind me while I am washing my hands.

I go over to the picture window when I leave the restroom. The same wispy clouds. I check the weather forecast on my phone again: "Clear and sunny skies." I pour a cup of coffee and walk slowly down an aisle past a bin full of overripe melons. I pick up a cellophane-wrapped pack of baseball cards, 1950s vintage, and study them front and back. It's hard to believe that the owner feels comfortable displaying them out on an open shelf. I pick through a stack of baseball caps beside them, no team east of the Mississippi.

I fetch a pint of chocolate milk from the cooler and open it on the way back to the counter. I ask the ghost-grey counter clerk his take on the weather, about going up through the pass and over.

"Yesterday was murder," baritone voice and a nod, eyes clear and earnest. "Haven't heard no complaints from people coming through today."

That's enough for me. I pull on my gloves before heading out and hold the door for a well-dressed couple to enter. She stops midway to let him know that "all men marry up." He smirks as he passes by, and whispers.

"Just in case you hadn't noticed."

The sky is clear back out at the gas pump. I stop at the driveway entrance to let a station wagon full of kids pull in. The driver is laughing, and the woman next to him.

There's no foreplay here. I power through a long curve, then directly up a steep straightaway. I downshift through a sharp bend and directly into another long straightaway. I am up into the hills in minutes, thoroughly chilled by the sudden ascent. I am shivering by the time I break over the first ridge into an entirely cloudless sky. This is going to be a beauty.

The cold becomes tolerable under the midday sun.

The road takes over, more cruise than challenge, great sweeping loops and rises around snow-strewn peaks and overhangs, past lookouts over October-decorated juniper and pine. I slow to soak up as much as I can, pull over when someone wants to pass.

Yesterday's hurricane is today's cold breeze, dusting me with a shimmer of snow blown off the high branches. I throttle my way through an occasional narrow, but mostly glide and sweep and glide some more. I am into shocking yellow aspens now, pulling off to capture their brilliance with my iPhone.

Cold comes to get me when the clouds roll in. I throttle up around the huge bald summit, then dip down the backside, downshifting to slow, a whine and purr, a string of hairpins and straightaways.

What matters most is that it is getting warmer.

Warmer still when I break out into an open bowl of green, scattered farms with whitewashed fencing, lush pastures and furrowed fields. I pull off onto the shoulder, get off, and sprawl on a grassy embankment. I zip open my jacket and luxuriate in the sun, for a while, stillness only.

I motor into a tourist town late in the afternoon. Eat here, sleep there, several signs to Durango on the far side of town. I pull into a gas station to check pressure at the computerized tire pump in the parking lot. Good thing, because my rear tire is low, acceleration through two days of curves.

The road to Durango is as good as it gets. Shallows and rises and long easy sweeps through old timber forest and pastureland. I throttle up inclines sprinkled with late season flowers, pass the shadowy profiles of grazing deer. I turn on my brights to warn them I'm coming. They are out in the open now, crossing the road in twos and threes. Another motorcycle ride at dusk.

I break out onto a pastured plateau, pass a falling down house and change my mind, swing around at the next intersection and head back. I park on the shoulder out front, hop a ditch and squeeze through a barbwire fence. I wade through the prickers in an overgrown yard to look into the dark openings of windows and doors. I step through a doorway onto the curled remains of a linoleum floor, feel my way across to a gaping door, then back out into the main room. An ancient woodstove is tipped onto its rusted side. Stories to tell, but no one's talking.

I look up through what's left of the roof beams, hear a yelp out behind the house. I listen for what does not come.

It's time to move on.

I go out past the pine tree in front of the house, stooping to angle between the wires, bounding over the ditch and across the road to my bike. I climb on, push the ignition, squeeze the clutch and shift, make a smoother than usual U-turn in the direction of Durango.

It is cooling off, but not enough for the bugs to disappear. They tick off the top of my helmet and splatter against my visor. I pass a bloated deer off the side of the road, neck twisted back against her ribcage. I drive on, haze leaking out from under the bushes, a smiling raccoon in a dark pool of blood welcoming the night with an upturned paw. My own sturdy roof having worn away, tears and a fogged-up visor.

There is light on the underside of the clouds ahead, a train whistle, the promise of a meal and a bed. The unearned gift of even a moment does not ensure a next.

There's a shock of stillness when I switch off the ignition, an honest weariness that feels like accomplishment. A ride beyond the contraction of fear.

Enough of the road, over-focus, contraction. I am ready for people and a plateful of something. I walk down the street to a brewery restaurant. The place is jumping for a Sunday evening, an hour-long wait for a table.

I wedge myself onto an open seat at the bar and order a draft and chicken stew. I drape my jacket over the back of the swivel chair and head for the restroom. I lather my hands and forearms before splashing water on my face. There's nothing I can do with my helmet hair, but that doesn't stop me from trying. Though road time is hacking away at the need to impress, there's still plenty to go around. The least I can do is laugh.

I get caught in an aisle behind a show-stopping young woman, torn jeans and tight among her less conspicuous companions. She is lovely. But if it is whimsical to pretend physical beauty doesn't matter, it's boxcar stupid to think it matters most. And I know something about stupid.

There's a barrage of conversation back at the bar. I'm spooning the stew but listening also. Off to my left an animated "Ain't going back there, man. No fucking way. Crazy ain't criminal." It's bracing, but less than invitational.

I take a swallow of beer and swing slightly to my right, unintentionally into a conversation between two middle aged women, something about astrological signs.

"You must be a Pisces," and we're off, a little too much interest in what makes me a Sagittarian. I'm back into the stew when the more reserved of the two excuses herself and saunters off to the restroom. Her wide-eyed friend leans in and playfully nudges my shoulder.

"Do you think I'm pretty?" When I have no quick response to her admirable directness, she winks. "Cat got your tongue?"

"A bit. And yes, you're very pretty. And I'm pretty old."

She pulls back as if I had rebuffed her and says nothing until her friend returns.

I get my check and pay, stand up to pull on my

jacket.

"Nice talking to you ladies," to which she leans over, eyes Doberman cold, and whispers.

"You old guys are so easy. All we have to do, really, is notice you." I have no answer, just a nod and a strained smile.

I'm more than a little confused when I get out on the street.

What did I do?

What could I have done differently?

I take a walk to clear my head. I don't come up with any easy answers, only a deepended discomfort with the aristocracy of beauty, the uneven and unearned quality of it. Not beauty itself, but what we have done with it. The pinched definition, the overvaluation and manipulation. Most of all the casualties.

It's a club I don't want to belong to.

I head down main street toward my bike. The flicker of a candle behind a gauzy second-floor curtain makes a mockery of my chosen aloneness.

On my way up the street to a string of inexpensive motels, I swing impulsively into a 7-Eleven for something sweet. I have a longstanding weakness for miniature chocolate doughnuts, the ones which would survive a millennium in a landfill. Sadly, they are out of chocolate. I settle for their powder-sugared sisters and put them in a plastic bag for easy passage on my bike. Rather than tucking them into a jacket pocket, I grip the bag to the throttle for the short run to a motel. The bag quickly inflates when I exit the driveway and pull up to the corner to turn. Distracted, I stop too quickly, lose my balance and tumble over. I'm okay, but I've banged up my bike.

"Damnit, John," and to my bike, "I'm sorry."

I try unsuccessfully to lift the Honda upright, setting off spasms in my back. I yank off my helmet and almost toss it, then walk out into the cross street to flag down some help. It arrives almost immediately in a muffler-less pickup that roars by and swerves to a stop. Two young men jump out and hurry back, asking how they can help in broken English. The three of us hoist the bike upright and walk it to the side of the road. I settle it on its kickstand and thank them for stopping. They smile and nod, "no problem, Mister," and will not accept the twenty I extend. Then they are back in their pickup and gone.

Whatever I have done to body and bike, I have crushed the donuts. I walk back to the store for reinforcements and add a carton of skim milk to the mix. The moderation of balanced excess. Gratitude gradually crowds out self-recrimination, eases the pounding in my chest.

I park my cycle under a light at the motel. I sign in and haul my gear to the room before coming back to inspect it. The turn-signal housing is split wide open, the rearview mirror a spiderweb of cracks. It's more evidence of my good standing in the clown brigade, in spite of the worthiness of the mission.

I search the sky for answers. Once again, I've screwed up, but the world has not ended.

Perfection remains well out of reach, but tape has always come through: scotch tape, duct tape, band aids and the like. I will get out the tape in the morning.

I check the clock on the end table. I have been in my powder-sugared bed for over an hour, successfully resisting the too-available TV. Apparently, the evening is not done with me. There is more to learn, or stew until I do. I have given up trying to make sense of the drama at the restaurant. Dropping the Honda is another matter. Coming on the heels of the storm in the mountains, it refuses to let go.

Is this decline or the brink of a precipitous fall?

I am seventy-four years old. Am I too vulnerable for mistakes, too glib in my dismissal of those suggesting that I act my age?

On the other hand, I fell down and I'm ok. Why let age degrade my well-exercised capacity for curiosity and adventure? Is extension as dangerous as shrinking my life under the guise of "being realistic"? Isn't there a price to be paid at the far end of life for what we *didn't* do?

CHAPTER 18

"HAVE YOU SEEN THE NEWS?" An abrupt question to wake to, and I say nothing.

"I'm sorry, did I wake you?"

"Yup, but that's okay. It's time to get up. What news?"

"About Las Vegas, the mass shooting."

"Mass shooting in Las Vegas?"

Barbara tells me about the guy with heavy weapons high up in a hotel, shooting down into an open air concert. Hundreds of people wounded or dead. I react with questions and exasperation, a sadness and madness we share.

"At least Kate and Nate are okay."

"Kate and Nate?" And then I remember the Las Vegas weekend they had planned with a group of their friends. "Were they still there?"

"In a plane on the runway when he started shooting."

———

It takes an hour to tape the turn signal in place, the shattered sections of the rearview mirror. Then I motor down into the city center and park. I spend a long time over coffee and a bagel, unable to pull myself away from the TV coverage streaming out of Las Vegas.

I take a slow walk down Main in the direction of the bookstore, checking eyes and being checked by people on the street. We all seem subdued, processing our shared distress in private.

I stop for a light at an intersection. On the corner across from me a young man is holding a black and white "Repent" sign, swinging it back and forth in front of walkers, stopping to speak to anyone who shows interest. An assistant is circling him, filming his interactions.

Repent for what, I am wondering, the slaughter in Las Vegas? Our eyes meet and he holds the gaze. The light changes and I cross, neither of us looking away. I stop a few feet short of him, look up at his sign and take a deep breath. He steps toward me as if I were making an invitation.

"Are you a believer?" His eyes are a clear Nordic blue. "Do you have a relationship with Jesus Christ?"

"I'll answer if you do."

"Fair enough," he smiles, young enough to know the truth.

"How do you feel about assault weapons?"

"I'm a second amendment guy," with less of a smile. "Your turn," very earnest, not a hint of a smirk.

"I'm a big fan of Jesus, the primacy of love."

We leave it there, nods and forced smiles, and I walk on, uncomfortable with the ease we all have of confusing certainty with fact.

***

In spite of the dour circumstances, I am greeted warmly when I enter Marie's Bookstore.

"Welcome back, John," from a clerk who helped me two years ago. "I really enjoyed your book."

I am pleased he remembers, and liked *Sailing Grace*. I thank him, embarrassed at not remembering his name. We catch up for a while and mull over Las Vegas. Then he gives me a tour of recent books about the Southwest. I take my time sampling, then buy one that most captures my interest. The forced economy of traveling by bike.

I return to the scene of last night's confusion and sip a beer at a table in the sun outside. I have the luxury of time in a town I love, and a new book that takes me in quickly. I finish the beer and take the book back to my bike, yawning and stretching, in need of exercise. Ignoring a complaining right knee, I take a sweaty hike up to Fort Lewis College on the bluff above the city. The college bookstore is closed by the time I arrive there, an hour before sunset.

I head off down a trail through a nearby stand of trees. Isn't there a clearing at the end of every path? There is no clearing. I turn back when the trail angles down into a muddy mess and stop when a breeze rattles the aspens to life. In among the shimmering others there's a tree twisted and torqued by lightning, startle and shock, an early death. I move on slowly, the weight of today's savagery, fierce canvas on which to limn beauty.

I watch the sun set over the mountains across the valley. Two hawks circle playfully in the deepening blue. Someone is playing an organ down in the city. The sound rides up on a freshening breeze, a melancholy incompleteness, almost a dirge.

We all live on death row. Only our exit dates differ. Most days I am at peace with dying, but in no particular rush. I'd like to die young, but just as late as possible, and greet death with open arms.

———————

I take the long way back to the city center, past a clapboard church with a come-to-Jesus chorus, welcome offset to my Last Vegas blues. Further on TV light dances on the curtains of a home, the squealed delight of a family laughing together.

I am thoroughly chilled by the time I get back downtown. I am also hungry. Like a junkie I decide to take my chances at the same brewery I went to last night. It seems unlikely I'll run into the astrologer and her friend.

Hesitancy builds as I approach the place, timidity probably a more accurate word. I remind myself that there is no such thing as invented wisdom. Only *found* wisdom, often discovered in situations of turmoil or pain. I'm feeling no need for either.

I stop at the doorway to let two middle age guys walk out, "Feeling my age" as they pass. I can turn around but don't. I am relieved to see no familiar faces when I enter.

I get a table at the back, entirely out of the social whirl. If anything the volume is louder tonight, incongruous on the day after a mass shooting. Perhaps it's an alcohol fueled remedy for distress. I go back to chicken stew and an amber, a rut sure enough, but one likely to satisfy. The stewy warmth ushers me down into my body, recess from an overheated brain.

The waitress brings two peanut butter cups with the check. I hand her my credit card and she disappears. I remove the foil wrapper without looking down, nodding to a scrutinizing couple a few tables away. I pop the peanut butter cup into my mouth and bite down, chagrined to find that I haven't removed it from the paper cup. *Too cool, old man,* depositing the gooey mess in the palm of my hand. *Way too cool.*

I go to the restroom before leaving, pass a gangly

young man running his hands up and down between the hot air blades of a fancy hand dryer. After doing my business I wash my hands and wait behind him. He keeps running his hands up and down, a trance of some sort before his high-frequency god. I don't want to interrupt whatever is going on, dry my hands on my shirt and head out the door.

I walk along the river on the way back to my bike, watching what look like seagulls floating downstream. They disappear beneath a bridge, then fly upriver to begin again.

I am entertained by the likelihood that I am not getting wiser with age, only deluded enough to confuse the two.

CHAPTER 19

I CALL Barbara before setting out in the morning. I am feeling uneasy, the aftertaste of Saturday's storm, the possibility of strong evening winds. I string out a playful recital of foibles and hesitations.

"You're the only area of my life not in need of an upgrade."

"I think that's a compliment," she replies.

"Know it."

I walk around the block before climbing on my bike. What a gift I have in Barbara, the animal energy she calls up in me, the drive and dare, the raw love of life.

Fear and love don't get along, a good thing because of my capacity to awfulize about the forecasted wind out in wide open Utah.

The road out of Durango is billygoat nirvana, inclines and descents, loops and swaybacks, slopes splashed with October-bright aspen. Ecstasy ends abruptly when I downshift too far on a steep downward drop, swerving slightly when my rear wheel catches and slides. *Attention, Johnny, beauty or not.*

I pass the turnoff to Mesa Verde National Park, will save it until I can return with Barbara. The road eases gradually downward and straightens, green going tan out in the distance.

I stop for a pint of milk in a small town and study the map while I drink it. Most of the roads ahead are two laners, sprinkled with those alternative routes that have earned my caution. Too often they are worn and uneven, gravelly in the curves, pitted and potholed and generally unfriendly. Not where I want to spend my time.

I will wander down into northern Arizona and rest for a while before angling north into Utah.

I motor through the first of a day-long string of Native American reservations. The green mountains have long surrendered to scrub grass and sand, gas stations, casinos, and mobile homes. Raggedy yards come alive with the squeals of high-octane kids. A fallen down sign for a cosmetology college points wistfully to the sky. A mattress leans against a barbwire fence. An EMT screams by, calling me to attention. There are way too many crosses by the side of the road.

I pass signs for touristy "Four Corners," where Colorado, New Mexico, Arizona and Utah intersect. I turn west onto a road that tells its own sad story, broken asphalt and ruts, a roadbed of sand. The washboard ride makes a mockery of the speed limit, thirty miles of tar patching for ten miles of road. It's not the kind of road you'd find in fashionable Santa Fe.

Distinctly non-governmental signs for unfenced livestock call up images of my grandfather Dunn. A family of cattle drovers my mother called them, true or imagined, real to me. Real also the first small herds of skinny cattle straggling onto the road. They look up languidly as I approach and take their time clearing the way.

I pass a huddle of what I hope are livestock sheds, tarpaper protection from sun and wind. What nineteenth century fencing did to the natives who lived here, destroying the travel routes of nomadic tribes whose only clock was seasonal. Forced reservations sealed the deal, leaving them dependent on pick-ups if they can afford them. Nothing about this is okay with me, but nobody is asking.

Just thinking about it gets me drifting across the centerline and into the oncoming lane. There's no exemption for high-minded thinking out here, a pothole away from a big surprise.

I turn north in the early afternoon, desert in every direction. Maybe it will be cooler up in Utah. I swerve in a curve when an overheated tar patch gives way under my back tire. No damage done, but it leaves me shaky. I slow as I pass a well-disguised turnout, a fifty-gallon drum and a scatter of beer cans, bird-skewered garbage bags and what looks like a sink.

It's getting hot in spite of the first stirrings in the air. I decide against stopping to climb out of my jacket. Although there's no sign of a windstorm, there are a few dust plumes out to the southwest.

I slow as I approach a truck upside down off the side of the road, its front tire lolling in the breeze. It's a rusted old thing, porous from generations of target practice. The pockmarked carcass of a corroded water heater snuggles up to a cactus a short way beyond.

I stop for air conditioning and water the next chance I get, leave my jacket and helmet in the sun to dry. I stand in front of the open meat counter inside, enjoying the chill on my sweaty shirt. I get water and milk from the cooler, pay and return to the refrigerated display. The sullen counterman hedges when I ask him about a well-publicized shootout between police and home-grown terrorists a few years back.

"Don't know much about those boys, 'cept they just disappeared out in the canyonland." It seems clear that he doesn't want to discuss it. "Just disappeared" over his shoulder as he moves by me to reload the cooler with a clatter.

I go to the restroom, remove my shirt and soak it under the coldwater faucet. I ring it out and put it back on, shuddering from the shock.

He is back behind the counter when I come out and head for the door.

I hesitate when he tells me "Be careful out there. The wind and all," when I look his way.

I pass through a bubble of coolness on a long straightaway climb a half hour later, and turn in at a gas station near the top. I buy yogurt and a bottle of water, ask about the road that angles off to the northwest.

"A real beauty if you like canyons."

"I do."

"Then you'll like it a lot. Quite a ways to the next town, so you'd better fill up."

I go out to the pump and top off, then back inside for a second bottle of water.

"You be safe out there in the wind."

The wind again.

I stand by my bike and take a reading. I developed some confidence about estimating the wind during years at sea on a boat without a working wind indicator. It's the kind of confidence that can get you in trouble. The breeze is beginning to kick in, enough in gusts to blow a nearby hammock sideways, a Utah spinnaker in the afternoon glare.

I turn onto the canyon road and slow when I pass the empty shelves of a pottery stand. There's a carpet of bright colored shards beneath it, and questions that ride with me the rest of the day.

The road dives down into a string of rose-colored canyons, sandstone up to silhouetted ridgelines, green along the river. I try to keep my eyes on the road. It has more than a few skid marks out over the centerline, drivers taken in by the beauty. That's not a track I want to take. Beauty or not, there's no room for wandering attention. I'll save that for my return with Barbara, seat-belt secure in wrap-around metal.

I pull off the road soon after breaking out of the canyons into what is most certainly not a ten-knot wind. Not even close. I am at sea again in an unforeseen front, battening down the hatches. I keep my back to the wind while cinching the bungies, tucking any wind-catching thing in tight. I moisten my lips and scan the horizon, flatland only and the taste of dust. I can do this, I remind myself, backhanding grit away from the corners of my eyes. I've been here before, on that other sea. I search my pockets for eye drops and find none. Just stay at the helm and muscle through. There's no alternative really, nowhere to hide.

Back on the road, I hunch down like a jockey, the Honda more racehorse than machine. I fight to stay off the shoulder in gusts, off the centerline when they let go. It's slow going, down to thirty-five, but I'm mostly staying between the lines.

The wind is raking the flats of every unattached thing. Like wind driven spray at sea, only tumbleweeds now and – did that just happen? – a sheet of green plastic roofing off somebody's shed, a dog in pursuit, paws barely touching the ground. I slow to thirty, but keep on going, wiggling my elbows back and forth to stave off cramping.

The wind eases somewhat in the valley approaching the Colorado River, further still after I cross it. The worst is over, fifteen dying knots now, the calm after a storm.

In the late afternoon I come up on signs announcing a town. There's nothing that looks like one, just a few weary farm buildings and a handful of cows gnawing at anything green. They freeze when they see me coming and stare as I whirl by. They look like statues in the rearview mirror.

A flash off the windshield of the first car I've seen in an hour reminds me to pay attention. I catch myself drifting again a short time later and start looking for somewhere to stop.

I pull off the first chance I get and park at what looks like a decent motel. It's a bit run down, but so am I. I remove my helmet and swipe dust off my jacket and jeans. I try to brush the dust off my face but end up just moving it around.

The motel manager takes one look at me and breaks into laughter. She tries to apologize, then tells me I look like a raccoon.

"But a fine-looking raccoon, I'm sure" gets her cackling again, turning away to catch her breath before turning back to me.

"What can I do for you?" cracks up both of us.

I resolve then and there not to inspect my room too closely. We are what we are, my room and I, and one of us is air conditioned.

I take a long shower in the rust-stained bathtub, cool at first to leech off the heat, then warmer to take off the chill. I dry off in front of a smudged mirror, enjoying the sandpaper surface of what's left of a towel. I pull on my flowered swimsuit and a tee shirt, and bundle my dusty clothes for the laundry. I pull on clean socks and my boots, grab a book, and lock the door behind me.

I get coins and detergent at the office and load up one of the surprisingly modern washing machines. It takes a while to figure out how to work it.

Then it's off in search of a meal, unsure how my outfit will play in Utah.

There's not much to see on the way to the restaurant. Empty storefronts raise questions about the town's well-being. I glance down a few dusty side streets lined with the one story bungalows so popular after the war. There's no sign of a school anywhere, so often the death knell of a rural town. No library, no police station, no post office in sight, a whole lot of no in a dusty town.

The restaurant looks almost out of place in its western polish. I am not confident about my shorts and boots, but hungry enough to give it a try. I am greeted, if that is the word, by a severe looking man with a greying crewcut and matching slacks. He glances down long enough to register disdain before taking a deep breath and picking up a menu. He walks me to the far end of the place. He places the menu on the side of a table that faces the wall, then turns on his heel and walks away.

I am too relieved with a seat and a menu to feel badly about the wall. I make a quick selection to cement the deal before my sober friend changes his mind. A waitress takes my order with the matter-of-factness of someone who's enjoying the host's consternation. She stops back with a beer and assures that my meal "will be out in a jiffy."

At the far end of a windblown day, the meal and the beer and the book and the wall are more than enough. On my way to the counter to cash out, a hulk of a man lumbers in like a bear, tugging at his grease-stained overalls. He looks me over, special attention to my shorts, and pats me on the shoulder with a paw of a hand.

"Very nice, young man," in a baritone voice. "Very nice indeed."

It is shockingly quiet outside, no lights to compete with the stars. The enormous unknowability of so much, the brilliance. I stand in the parking lot long enough for dinner warmth to sag into dead-dog tired. So tired I hardly register the man I pass further down the street. He is standing beside the open driver's side door of a car, urinating into the lighted interior. He looks my way and nods.

"The son of a bitch is screwing my wife." Nothing more.

I'm a goner by the time I get to the motel. I drop a handful of road clothes onto the laundry floor when loading the dryer. The door creaks open behind me while I'm gathering them up. I swing around to what looks like a mother and daughter.

"Don't let us bother you," the older one smiles. "Just checking out those flowered shorts."

It's a long way up the stairs, and when I get there, a short way to bed. I prop a pillow behind my head and click through the channels in search of politics or football. I settle on football in hopes it will keep me awake long enough to retrieve my clothes from the dryer.

When I eventually do, I can't help but glance with dumb-dog wonder at the bras and panties whirling around in the dryer next to mine.

I climb the stairs to my room and stop, elbows up on the balcony rail. I lean into the warmth of my clothes and the stillness, for a while more night than me.

CHAPTER 20

I SLIP into a space at the crowded breakfast bar in the morning, tucked in between two hulky truck drivers and the mother-daughter duo from the laundry room. Mom looks over her daughter's shoulder to let everyone know.

"See you've got your britches on this morning," before mercifully returning to the drama they're discussing.

"Biggest investment she ever made was lotto tickets at the party store. And him, if you're counting. Anything to ease the pain."

On the other side there's an homage to "my smartass kid," and the "fifty-mile gusts someone radioed about last night." They were nowhere near fifty but gust they did.

I break open the yolks of my poached eggs and spread their soft centers over the burnt hash browns. I take a sip of bold dark coffee with just a splash of cream.

I glance out to where my Honda is waiting and take another sip.

How did I get so lucky?

The road west snakes through giant clots of rock, then into crevices, ancient and alien, that compete with the road for my attention. I pull off on the grassy floor of a canyon when I sense movement up on a cliff wall. It takes a while to focus in on a procession of longhorn sheep on a narrow ridge, stopping to graze, then moving on. I feel something like vertigo just watching them.

I pass a series of official looking signs announcing sights and overlooks on a road to the south. I turn and begin an upward march on a narrow road along a spine of rock, bleached and barren panoramas on both sides of the road, canyon-pocked wasteland as far as I can see.

I pull into a tiny parking lot and stop. I am the only person here. I walk over to the edge of the cliff and settle down on a sturdy park bench. I look out for a while, the scorched and scoured emptiness, the wordless clarity of open space. I rest my tired eyes. My thinking gives way, awareness only, a deepening sense of being part of something larger.

I am back on my bike in the late afternoon. I lock my focus to the asphalt between the guard rails, off the throttle and gliding, looping down through the switchbacks, this way and that, pulling up at dusk to a small-town campground.

There are plenty of open sites for my cigar-size tent. It takes only minutes to pop it up. I am startled when I step back into a Paul Bunyan character who has wandered up behind me.

"No disrespect, Mister, but you actually sleep in that itsy-bitsy tent?"

"Yup."

"Shrimpy little thing, ain't it?"

"Yeah, but it fits on my cycle and there's less to heat."

"To heat?" And after a long pause, a baby-wide grin. "You kiddin' on me now?"

"Could be."

I beat the dinner rush, and park with a book at a corner table. I leave the book and reading glasses and go to the restroom. When I sit back down, I realize that I did not look in the mirror when washing my hands. Never thought of it. Is this progress or more evidence of deterioration? So much of whom I thought I was is falling away, leaving only who I am.

I order a spinach salad sprinkled with sliced strawberries. Aflush with righteousness, I snap a picture of it and send it to Barbara.

"It's called dinner," I tell her later. She responds with full throated laughter.

"That's my guy, the one with the salad."

We talk about her day, then mine, the beauty, my eroding sense of separateness.

"I think it's possible that 'other' is a game the brain plays with 'only'."

"You're gonna have to help me with that one, John."

"You know how the brain delivers experience in separate and discreet parts — for every here a there, every now a then — as if everything is separate from everything else. Man and nature, body and spirit, the list goes on. You and me, for that matter. We can think of ourselves as apart, miles and such, but are we really apart? Can we be apart?"

"I like that, John." She leaves it there. But not me.

"All I'm trying to say is that out here in these open places, it is harder to think of myself as separate from everything else. What seems more likely is that beneath the *this*ness and *that*ness I experience is a boundless *is*ness I share with you, everyone and everything. A less obvious but deeper level of reality."

"A version of what you've been thinking for a while."

"Yeah, but more obvious when I let go of all the thinking *about,* and just let the world rush in."

We make our way back through kids and the Michigan fall to an airline ticket for my trip home.

"I can't wait to get my hands on you."

I'm not ready to turn in yet. Not without an evening walk, another mile or two.

I bundle up and go out into the coldest night of the trip. What sounds like a clarinet calls me in the direction of a shadowy outcropping on the horizon. I walk down a street into a neighborhood of nondescript houses. Bright downstairs lights are giving way to softer ones upstairs. I stop at a quiet intersection, stoop down to pet two well-kept dogs leashed outside a lighted beauty shop. I look back a half block later, their heads pivoting in unison as they inspect a passing truck.

I walk through an aging business district, unsure how far I can ride the spinach and strawberries. They seem no match for this cold night. I round a corner to a neon-lit bar with a scatter of trucks out front. Music also, probably electronic, a warm glow through the windows. *Just a beer* I'm telling myself, but thinking *chips and cheese.*

I almost put my hand through a tired looking screen door I do not see. It's been pushed in and out so many times the brads are straining to hold it together. I have to wrestle with the oak door behind it, but eventually shove it open. It is warm inside.

A new face in town draws a few nods and a "make yourself at home" from the round-faced bartender. I sit down at the bar and order a local draft that – in spite of her insistence — is too hoppy by a lot. I console myself with a platter of chips and cheese, loaded up with raw onions that do nothing but please. Protection from freezing I assure myself, heat for my miniature tent.

I'm not interested in conversation this evening, quite happy with my quickly disappearing plate of chips. I can't help but overhear a conversation beside me, some version of "I was a real looker, believe it or not." Chuckling now, "Talk about investing in a depreciating asset."

As I get up to go, her mustached companion wraps a ham-sized arm around her and pulls her close.

It's freezing outside. I walk as fast as my heart will let me. The clarinet has long gone off to bed, replaced in the light-eating sky by the first hint of a moon. With every lost degree another degree of stillness, always more difficult within myself.

CHAPTER 21

I SHIVER AWAKE several hours later. I thrash around in my sleeping bag to generate warmth, then try to fall back to sleep. In a short time I'm shivering again, trembling I can't control. Sleep is out of the question.

I work myself out of the sleeping bag, slip into my boots, grab my dew-soaked bike bag and head for the restroom. Fortunately, it is heated. I pull on thermal underwear and socks, fleece pullovers, and a wool hat. When I am warm, I retreat to the tent and burrow into my sleeping bag. I am awake again before daylight, cold but not dangerously so.

I crawl out into sunlight at 7:00 A.M., less than rested but ready for coffee. Campers are beginning to stir around me, waving their arms and hugging themselves to generate some heat.

"A cold one," somebody shouts. "Down into the thirties."

What D.H. Lawrence was referring to with his "hard heat or hard chill" description of the Southwest.

I order a bagel and raspberry yogurt, and a very welcome cup of coffee. I gulp them down and go back for seconds. Replenished, I wash up and pull my gear together, then study a map on the office wall. I have studiously avoided the "must see" sights on this trip, saving them for when Barbara and I return. I'm more interested in unnoticed places and the people who live there. I plan to skirt the edges of Bryce Canyon and Zion national parks on my way south today, more a glance at the menu than a full course meal.

The first hours take me on a hallucination tour of canyonland, a climb so spectacular that I regularly slow to let others pass. My neck tires from swiveling between asphalt, sandstone, and the azure sky. Up and down and around I go, split screen attention to the road and these gods of rock, red stone gone white over eons in the sun, then dive down through seams of sandstone and lime into green-floored gorges full of shade.

I stop in one of these to confer with two horses grazing behind a split-timber fence. They saunter over to the edge of the corral, the illusion that I'm packing carrots. They hang their huge heads over the rail and linger, fleshen allies among the rockage. They let me caress their muscled jawlines, run my fingertips down between their eyes. I talk to them, but they say nothing, their silence like the language of God.

I drive on more slowly than before, from sunblind vistas down into valley cleavage where furnace heat makes it hard to draw a breath. I enter the compression of a national park, clots of cars and campers on narrow roads, an almost claustrophobic sense of suffocation, a swelling need to break out. I resolve to bring Barbara back to see this, but only at dawn or dusk.

I don't want to let the traffic crowd out awe. I settle into a slow procession up striated rock faces, red to tan to white near the top, shelves and spires, a rare waterfall, spiny stone sculptures and stand-alone towers. Saw-toothed ridgelines and promontories become more available when I stop to gawk from a ledged parking lot.

I follow my iPhone around for a while, trying to capture what cannot be contained. I give up at some point and go back to gazing. This is it, John. Don't miss it.

Tour buses roll in one after another, disgorging their sun-shocked oldsters. Sighs and smiles and camera clicking, a vivid flashback for their motorcycling companion.

For a few minutes, I am a less than enthusiastic five-year-old, captive of old aunts at a family gathering. Trapped of course but curious also, drooping petticoats and opaque compression stockings, the availability of veins and knuckles through almost transparent skin. I am too young and dumb to appreciate the earned quality of their lives, what they have endured and survived and learned from, just sitting as they do and smiling, peppering me with questions about my small life.

Today they give me parking lot absolution, seem delighted to have me linger. They welcome my questions and attention, smile forgiveness for what I missed seventy years ago.

———

Shadows are deepening now, traffic thinning. I coast down a red-powdered road into a valley's long stretch of shade. Then it's out into the open, across rose-hued flats and up again, eventually spilling down into wine-dark expanses sprinkled with sturdy pinyon pine. I know I'm not paying attention when I get used to any stable thing.

I take a break at a dilapidated rest stop, to stretch and walk around. The overflowing trash cans are in need of relief, shreds of litter dancing off on a welcome breeze. I retrieve what I can and cram it down into the containers. The wind picks up and the dance begins again. This is no place to relax. I get back underway, pass a decaying Volkswagen van. The past is rich, but it's not where I'm headed.

I pass a caved-in bridge on an abandoned access road, concrete remains scattered on the bone dry riverbed. Not a mile further an almost green hillside makes its way up to where the aspen take over. The views argue against dozing, but I am slipping in that direction. I pull off the next chance I get, into a faded gas station in an intersection town. A worn-out old dog is sprawled in the shade out front. He is a patchy mess, shaggy in a few places, hairless in others. He seems long past barking or whining. Our eyes meet as I gas up, but he doesn't even lift his head. He does work his way up onto his paws when I finish and move toward the door. I drop to a knee and we have a one-sided conversation during which he settles back on his haunches. There is no glimmer in his eyes.

I go inside to ask about a restroom. The woman behind the counter puts her ear up to the holes drilled in the bullet thick plexiglass that divides us. I ask again, louder this time, and she points over her shoulder and shouts.

"Out there."

"Thank you," I shout back.

I'm feeling no urgency. I am hot and the air conditioning feels good. I take my time in front of the open cooler before settling on an iced coffee and a quart of water. I stop before a display of everything Jerky and grab a double pack of dried beef sticks. I wave them in front of the encased clerk and nod out in the dog's direction.

"Okay for the pooch?" I shout, and she smiles warmly.

"He'd love them," she shouts back.

A skinny teenage boy with thick glasses moves by her in the cage and begins to refill the cigarette case behind her. Annoyance gathers at the corner of her mouth, a younger brother I'd guess. I slide a bill into a slot in the plexiglass and gather up the change she passes back. We've given up shouting. We smile and I take my wares outside.

The dog doesn't thank me, only leans in to gnaw at the beef jerky sticks. I fluff his matted fur while he eats, then stand up and gulp down the water. I pop the top off the coffee on the way to the restroom. The sign above the toilet in the entirely chartreuse bathroom reads "The road ahead lies within," not your standard men's room fare.

I finish the iced coffee out at the bike, glancing back to the station window where the clerk inside is watching. I smile and nod my goodbye, and she gives me a wave. How impossible it is to know another person, no matter the time we are given. What a shame not to try.

I stay too late in the hills, transfixed by the hawks wheeling in the updrafts above the cliffs, the bats entering the insect-laden dusk. What I'm watching might seem ordinary to the locals. It does not seem ordinary to me. I climb back on my bike wondering if anything really goes unobserved.

It is early evening now, grazing time for critters. I fall in behind a van on the way to St. George, a shield between me and any road-crossing thing.

I pull into a gas station on the outskirts of town. It must be closing time somewhere. There's a pickup scrum out at the gas pumps, a stampede to the glass doored coolers inside. Twelve packs are a hit at the cashier's counter, an occasional fussy six pack of bottles. A sunbaked few go straight for the twenty-four ouncers, removing the caps before settling up. The day is not done. Let the games begin.

While I'm standing in line with my sorry little bottle of water, a shiny black hearse rolls up out front, the casket inside highlighted by the setting sun. Two young men in dark suits jump out and rush in, leaving their doors open behind them. They head straight for the cooler, the lead guy doing the talking.

"He don't care. He's not going anywhere."

I use an app the kids have installed on my phone to locate a nearby motel. Three stars for a bargain price it tells me, even a map to get there. I roll into the motel parking lot in less than ten minutes and lean back against my cycle to call Barbara before it's too late. The Honda's heated engine ticks down as we talk, her day and mine, my excitement about coming back here together. Being apart ratchets up the warmth we have for each other.

"Soon," I assure her, "after I store the cycle in Encinitas."

"A couple of days?"

"A couple of days. But first, Death Valley."

I lug my gear to the room and click on the TV to speculation about the Las Vegas shooter's motivation. I sort clothes and camping gear into separate piles, then re-sort the clothing for the remaining days of heat. I will pack everything I'm not likely to use in the bottom of the bike's saddle bags.

I am chilled by the time I get to the shower and scrub off in water that is almost hot. I shave and slip into clean clothes for the evening, go to the front desk to ask about restaurants.

"I'd like to walk," earns me a vacant stare, and when that doesn't work, "What would you recommend?"

"Just food, or something to drink?"

"A cold beer would be good."

"There's Italian up the street. Or some mighty good Mexican in the other direction."

"They both sound good. Thank you." I take a free USA Today from the counter.

"It gets a little wild at the Tex-Mex joint," as I turn to go.

I find my way to an uninspired plate of Mexican, too aware of the blue-jeaned clubsters who saunter by. I've been away from Barbara too long.

It's important to know what's going on in the world, but I tend to overdo it. My appetite for information is clearly part of my trouble with attention. That doesn't get in the way of overgrazing the sports section after practically memorizing the first section.

I order a celebratory dessert and sample the entertainment section while drenching myself in dark chocolate. I've been away from anything resembling bright lights for a while, and am reintroduced quite graphically to celebrity power, the fascination with anything that distracts. I put down my fork and ask for the bill.

I take the bill and a credit card to the counter, where the cashier and shift manager are deep in discussion.

"Just because I'm pretty doesn't mean I'm not psycho."

"Pretty can be pretty crazy," he nods, directing her attention to me.

She swipes my card vigorously before announcing "It's not taking." That's not good. I am living off this card.

"Try to run it through more slowly," the manager suggests. To my great relief, it takes on the second try.

I take a long walk then stop in a parking lot to do some stretching. Two kids in floppy shorts stop to watch.

"Hey Mister, whatya doing?"

"Stretching. Sore back."

"Huh," and one of them tries it. "Easy."

"Used to be," holding a stretch and smiling, "a long time ago."

"You keep at it, old man," fairly bouncing now as he heads off down the street. "You keep it up."

I try unsuccessfully to suppress my laughter, warm with affection for the world.

I stop abruptly on the walk back to the motel, startled at a ruckus in the bushes across the road. A shriek now, meal and mauler. Silence.

"Beauty and terror," Rilke whispers. How to stay in the fray, both engaged and serene, something I have never been good at.

CHAPTER 22

SLEEP RUNS out of patience with dark chocolate at daylight. I take a melatonin and wait for it to ease me back to sleep. It doesn't.

I drag myself out of bed a little before seven and load up the bike while it is still cool outside. I stuff myself at the breakfast smorgasbord and dawdle over the morning newspaper long enough to saturate myself with coffee.

I catch a glimpse of my father in a full-length mirror on my way to the parking lot. I'm reminded of his head-wagging amusement at my antics, his eyes and enveloping smile. I laugh out loud moments later when my boot catches on the cycle seat, what time and miles have done. I hope you're enjoying this, Dad.

The mountains recede as I cross a thin slice of Arizona and descend into Virgin River Gorge. The road plunges down between overhanging cliffs so stunning that only fear keeps my eyes on the road.

The canyon spills out into a pale green valley, mountains to the south, and far to the west the cloud-spackled splendor of the desert. The hills bleed color as I descend, going almost monochromatic as I bottom out in the purgatorial heat of the Nevada flats. Sign after sign announces the distance to Las Vegas, as if encouraging drivers to hang on.

I watch what looks like wildfire smoke out over the road ahead. Drivers are pulling off and climbing out of their cars with their cameras. Motorcycle riders also, one gesturing frantically at the spiral of smoke wobbling toward us. I ease off the throttle and touch the brakes, then realize the smoke is really dust. The funnel veers across the road ahead of me, gusting as I pass.

Las Vegas rises out of the desert an hour later, tempting me to stop. It's not why I'm out here, I remind myself, although not without some hesitation. I stay on the highway through the heart of the city, past the golden façade of the Mandalay Bay Hotel. To my amazement, the curtains are still blowing out of the windows from which the killer sprayed carnage on the concert goers below. It feels like riding through a nightmare.

I try to stay clear of the drifting lanes of freeway gawkers, and exit south of the strip onto a state road to the west. I follow it through the billowing suburbs, sagebrush and condominiums and cranes. Beyond that, thirsty country, generous with sunshine, stingy with shade. An occasional unhealthy looking cactus clings to the ground, prickly and flowerless, or gnarled to the point of grotesque. Every living thing has gone leathery, like the reptiles who only surface at night.

I pull off for gas at an isolated station, haunted by stories of station-less deserts. Two dogs are playing war out by the pumps, a third howling in a crouch off to the side.

"C'mon guys," I complain, but they're having none of it.

I ask a man at the next pump for the best road into Death Valley. I have no idea what he tells me, only the earnestness with which he tries. I will find my way. He will travel with me, all eagerness and intent.

On the outskirts of Pahrump, I come up behind a pickup piled with furniture. I give him a lot of room as the furniture looks unstable. A semi grinds up behind me, trapping me in place. I pull out enough to check for oncoming traffic, then blow by the overloaded truck just as furniture begins tumbling off the back. In my mirror I see pieces of rubber peeling away from the semi's left tire. The two of them ease off the road behind me in a synchronized cloud of dust.

There are oversized signs on the road through Pahrump, but not a lot to back them up. I am excited to see what a late afternoon sun does to Death Valley and decide against stopping for the night. I pull into Taco Bell before moving on.

I drive up the gravel entranceway, park, and go inside. It is surprisingly modern and air conditioned in the extreme. I order a bean burrito and an oversized cup of ice water and take them to a table with a window. I watch a ragged-looking man in the driveway outside, trying to stop cars before they pull out onto the road. He is asking for help with an extended hand, thin pickings in this suffocating heat. With his genes and journey, would I be standing anywhere else?

I go to the restroom before leaving, lock the door and remove my shirt. I fill the sink and soak it in cold water, wring it out and put it back on. Two white-collared business types give me a stern looking over when I pass them out in the parking lot.

I dig out a bill on my way to the man standing at the foot of the driveway. He nods and smiles when we shake hands, his eyes rimmed with weariness and red.

"Thank you for stopping." He does not look down to check.

"You're most welcome," so little when he needs so much.

Back at the bike, I pull my jacket over the wet t-shirt,

road protection from the moisture-sucking heat. Then my helmet, visor open, chin strap tight. The engine catches quickly and I swing by the restaurant as he comes around the building and heads for the door.

"Bless you, brother" he shouts.

"You too, man."

I turn off the state road in a few miles, down a resurfaced straightaway into a yawning basin, more caldron than the seabed it used to be. It's an incinerator now, fragments and ashes, no water, no shelter, unsurvivable heat and cold. A death of a place, bleached almost white, how can I find it so beautiful?

I drive for a long time before a smudge appears in the heatwaves, still longer for the hard angled outlines of something man-made. I come to a sign announcing "Death Valley Junction." I drive through what must have been a town and turn into a cinder-floored square of ancient buildings. I circle it — no sign of life — park, climb off and stretch my legs. In among the deserted buildings is one advertising itself as the "Amargosa Opera House." Try as I might, I can't make sense of an opera house out in the middle of nowhere.

Thoroughly bewildered, I just start laughing. Isn't this, weird as it seems, exactly what I wanted? Some time out beyond everything I call normal, the unfiltered rest of it, heat and wind and off-centered others, even the thinning identity I hold to be me, uncoupled for a while from history and association, this swelter of a place out in empty, mystery and beauty, naked awareness.

I turn left the next chance I get, onto pavement so fresh it seems incongruous, laid across the almost lunar landscape, bone white going almond in the late afternoon sun. A smolder for Jesus and those anchorite boys, to burn away every non-essential thing. Less a place to live than die.

Further on, a thin string of rock reaches out for the horizon, taking my eyes to a dark spot dancing in the hallucinatory haze. As the miles melt away, the spot gets darker, metastasizing into a cluster of dots, then dump trucks and earth movers and helmeted humans.

I slow down a good way off, eventually easing to a stop behind a dusty pickup. There's a shiny sedan ahead of him and a construction worker with a stop sign pole in one hand and a walkie-talkie in the other. They are routing traffic down a single lane of fresh asphalt, traffic in one direction waiting for traffic in the other to pass. There's more wait than traffic, which is fine with me. I stand up enough to get my butt off the seat, stretch and breathe, reach behind me for a thermos of water. I take several long swigs and slide it back under its bungee.

In time a truck with flashers comes toward us, and

behind it a car and truck. He pulls off to the side to let them pass, then swings around into position in front of us. The signal woman swivels her sign from "stop" to "slow" and we're off. It's five o'clock on Friday afternoon, and the lead vehicle is wasting no time. We accelerate up into the mid-forties along the smooth new lane, past asphalt spreaders and dump trucks, a string of pickups with construction workers standing out back, for the better part of a still-steaming mile.

The lead truck and sedan are way out ahead now, flashers disappearing over a rise. The driver in front of me is slowing for stretches, leaning over in the cab, almost out of sight, then sitting upright and accelerating hard, slowing to lean over whatever he is doing, then taking off again. I'm in no particular rush. I'm giving him a lot of room when he brakes abruptly, lurches violently to the left, leaning hard to follow him, off the end of the pavement now, flying, flying, until very suddenly I am not.

SURVIVE

"Let everything happen to you:
Beauty and terror.
Only press on."

Rainer Marie Rilke

"Ring the bells that still can ring.
Forget your perfect offering.
There is a crack in everything.
That's how the light gets in."

Leonard Cohen

CHAPTER 23

NOTHING.

A blue sky above.

My head cockeyed against my breath-fogged visor.

Something hot and sharp under me.

Someone leaning over me,

"Are you okay?"

Nothing. A second voice,

"Are you okay?"

"I think so," a convulsion of pain when I try to move.

"Don't move," and I stop. The pain doesn't.

I cough, a jagged stab of pain.

A sleepy stillness within which I contract, shuddering distress.

"Would you open my visor?" to someone I cannot see.

"Yes, but hold your head still."

Fresh air.

"Thank you."

An unfamiliar fullness in my chest when I inhale.

I reach for my chinstrap.

"Don't move," but I am moving, left arm first, and then my throbbing right.

I can move my fingers — damn that hurts — and wiggle both of my feet. I am not paralyzed.

I rock my head slowly, then attempt to lift it off the ground.

"Please take my helmet off."

After a brief discussion someone does, slowly, carefully, a second pair of fingers on either side of my face.

"Get something to put under his head," and in moments a rolled-up towel is worked under my head.

I roll my head again, slowly, this way and that. Deep relief.

I am neither dead nor paralyzed, but I am broken. And, as my head clears, anxious. It feels like my lungs are filling.

"I need to get up."

"You can't do that."

"Yes I can, and I need to. I'm not getting enough air."

People in the circle above me glance back and forth. No one says anything.

"I need to stand up. If I can't do it I'll lie back down."

Still nothing.

"Please. Help me get up."

An older man bends down and takes a knee beside me. He reaches out cautiously.

"Thank you. But not on that side. It will have to be over here on my left." He gets up, steps over me, and kneels back down. He looks up at the others for help. They step in around me, talking logistics.

"I'm going to need somebody to lift from behind, but only on my left side. "My right side's messed up."

Whatever doubts they have, they move in to assist.

I try to conceal the pain that rips through me as they help me to my feet. The blood accumulating in the sleeves of my jacket spills out onto my boots.

I try to draw a deep breath and can't, triggering a tortured spasm and a mouthful of mucus, which I spit out. Everybody but the man attached to my left elbow steps back. They try to protect me from their revulsion.

"Sorry about that," and looking down, "but there's no blood."

"That's good," somebody rallies, but all eyes are on me. I make a lame attempt to lift the mood.

"Got a few dented fenders, but the car still runs."

A few forced smiles, but not much eye contact. They probably think I've gone batty.

"Has anybody called for an EMT?" the older man asks.

"Tried to, but I don't have coverage."

After several people report the same, a young man sprints off toward his open-top Jeep.

"I'll drive back towards Pahrump, dialing 'til I get through."

I take inventory as I stand there, trying not to topple over or get too wrapped up in my pain. I can't draw a full breath, but if spit means anything my lungs aren't punctured. I can stand on my own, but I'm not sure about moving. I'm not bleeding badly given my medicinally thin blood.

Somebody over near the heavy machinery is waving his hands and shouting.

"An EMT is on the way."

There's a murmur in the growing crowd around me, whispering relief. I want to assure them I'm okay, but I'm clearly less than okay.

I look around. I'm standing in a field of rubble, chunks of rock the size of lemons on the jagged foundation of the road. My wounded bike is only steps away, handlebars torqued grotesquely under the frame, like a carcass on the road. I shuffle instinctively in that direction, sadness overriding pain. I am close to tears standing over her. She is banged up but intact. The key is dangling from the ignition, which someone has clicked off. *If I can get you started, we might make it to Encinitas.*

When my throttle hand tightens reflexively, blood is dripping off my fingers. I cannot raise my arm to stop it.

The old guy is still beside me, hand up under my left arm.

"We need to get you settled somewhere, to wait for the EMT."

"I'm better on my feet and moving."

"Let me track your vital signs at least, and do something about that bleeding." When I try to fend him off he persists.

"I'm a doctor." And when I look, "used to be a doctor. I don't practice any more. Mind's not up to it."

"Working well enough for me. Thank you."

Traffic is beginning to edge by, people slowing to see what's happened. The doctor and I move to the shoulder of the road, shepherded by several men who seem determined to see this through. They lift my bike upright and set it on its kickstand. They retrieve my helmet and the bike bag that ruptured when I crashed. Someone tears a towel apart. The doctor wraps pieces of it around my bleeding hands. Each is deeply gashed and swelling, furrows from the fingers up under the torn sleeves of my jacket. No one suggests removing the jacket, uncertain of what it's holding together inside.

We stand around like a group of teenagers might after a minor car accident, waiting for the police to arrive. I try to keep things light. The world doesn't end very often, that sort of thing. I am also talking to myself. They regularly check how I am doing.

"I'm okay so long as I can move around."

At one point the doctor insists that I sit down on my bike bag so he can check my vital signs. They ease me down. I sit for as long as I can. They help me up when I can no longer stand the pain.

Where's that EMT?

When they ask about the trip, I thoroughly embellish what can be embellished. Anything to keep the pain at bay. The adrenaline overdose is burning off, and my energy with it. Although the sun is still hot, I am beginning to shiver. I am also feeling queasy.

I step over to the edge of the road and study the desert. The sun that turns everything to leather during the center of the day is turning everything orange in decline. It is unspeakably beautiful. More powerful for knowing they will soon take me away. I am grateful and I am sad. It's like the end of an arduous ocean crossing, eagerness to arrive, awareness of what you're leaving.

Leaving as soon as possible, I hope, for I am getting weak.

"I'm ready to lay down now," I tell my companions. "Over here against this mound of sand, if you'll help me."

They seem relieved to get me off my feet, and eager to help me. The old doctor checks my pulse again.

"Steady, but pretty slow."

"Isn't slow good for a world class athlete?" I grin.

He tries his best to smile back.

The wail of a siren in the distance sounds like music to me.

The road crew closes the lane so the EMT can barrel through. It lurches to a stop on the road beside me. An intense young man in dayglo yellow bounds out of the vehicle and kneels down next to me. His assistant follows with a large medical bag. The young guy short-cuts through my identifying information and description of the accident. He follows with a series of diagnostic questions. He is not interested in detailed answers, or my weak attempts at humor. Yes and no will do.

He flexes a pair of industrial scissors, then curses under his breath when he can't cut through the canvas skin of my jacket. He changes to a pair of metal cutters, carving his way up the right sleeve and across my chest. When he pries the jacket open, shattered carbon plates spill out on the sand between us.

He rocks back on his heels and wipes the sweat out of his eyes. He scissors away my t-shirt and begins to examine me. He feels my swelling arm and shoulder, then down along my ribcage. He does not seem pleased.

"There's a lot of blood pooling in here, and I'm afraid a lot of breakage."

He shakes his head and grimaces.

"We'll get an IV going. And we're going to need a helicopter."

"Helicopter?"

He looks at me evenly, then at the scar down the center of my chest.

"Heart?"

"Yup."

"How long ago?"

"Twenty years."

He nods and leans in, speaking softly.

"I don't want to be disrespectful, Mister, but you're really busted up. We have to get you to a trauma hospital. And we don't have a lot of time."

I like this guy and trust him. I nod my assent.

"Call in a helicopter."

His assistant hands him a bag of IV fluid and bolts off to their rig.

There's a place for surrender and I do that, drifting away while he works over me. It is impossible that I will not hold Barbara again.

He rouses me to assure "they're on their way." He tells me it is important to stay awake. I nod off while he's talking and he wakes me again. He tells me they have to transport me back to the Junction for pickup.

"The hard part will be getting you onto a gurney," he warns me. "We'll try not to hurt you too much."

We are way beyond "too much" when they roll me onto my left side to work a sheet under me for lifting. I am not at all brave when they hoist me, convulsing uncontrollably when bone grates against bone, almost passing out. I am writhing again when we bump up onto the landing site a short time later.

I slip away, then come to as the helicopter spools up, amazed at how smoothly it lifts into the air. In and out of consciousness when we are underway, I wake with a start when a paramedic jerks away from me and shouts.

"Fire ants."

She and her partner are brushing them off me and stomping.

"Oh, no!" when she sees them crawling out of a bloody hole in my jeans. I am too sedated to be bothered that they're feeding on my knee.

I wake to hear a paramedic's oohing and aahing. I raise my head enough to see mountaintops glide by. They wake me again to get emergency information as the helicopter angles down toward the roof of the hospital. I give them Barbara's name and number, but insist they let me talk to her first.

"She needs to hear my voice, to know I'm okay."

I open my eyes to find three doctors working over me under a blinding light. They run through their diagnostic checklists, stepping away from the table to record their findings. One of them leans in to question me, dark smudges under her eyes. The pain is such and the heft of medication that I struggle to speak above a whisper. I try to answer her questions, but she cannot hear me. She leans in closer, ear above my mouth, but I cannot talk when the spasms come.

At some point they huddle to discuss a course of action. One of them outlines the sequence of x-rays and CAT scans, and the reason for each. When they've finished, I ask to phone Barbara first.

"So how are you doing?" to get her started, immediately buoyed by the excitement in her voice. She tells me about the talk she and Erin had over dinner and how much they are enjoying tonight's "chick flick."

"And how about you, Johnny Bob?"

"I'm okay." How to do this? "I had a great ride today, but it ended rather abruptly."

"That sounds a little ominous."

"I'm fine, Sweetie, but I did have an accident."

"Oh no!"

I can hear Erin in the background.

"What is it, Mom? Is Dad okay?"

"Tell Erin I'm okay. But I am in a hospital in Las Vegas getting checked out."

I share enough to take the worst case off the table,

but not enough to satisfy nurse Erin. Barbara will have to handle that.

We close with a plan. She will fly out in the morning, with or without our family nurse. Erin is insisting on coming, Barbara resisting. They'll work that out.

The doctors are gesturing impatience.

I try to end on a light note.

"You know that song about 'trusting your cape'?"

Silence.

"I might have overdone it this time."

CHAPTER 24

IT'S hard to remember I'm on pain medication when the radiology folks take over. Every move, every posture, sends me into spasms, stabbing so severe I almost pass out. This goes on deep into the night. A second round of x-rays and scans begin again at daylight, to answer questions raised by the first. I drift in and out of an almost hallucinatory stupor between tortured rounds in the radiology department.

I am accompanied at every step by a trauma nurse who spends the whole night on a chair next to my bed, calming my drugged agitation with a hand on my wrist. Trapped inside pain, I tether myself to the hand on my wrist.

Barbara arrives about noon, and with her, warmth and release. A doctor and nurse follow her into my room to do a second round of cleaning and assessing my wounds. They remove the temporary dressings and salves, deal patiently with my wincing and pulling away. They open the gouges on my hands as far as possible, and use q-tips to remove the gravel and debris they find. They talk as they work about damage to the tendons between my fingers. After excavating what they can, they medicate and re-bandage my hands. They turn their attention to my gouged knees and a tear under my ankle. I try to distract Barbara, who has trouble watching. We have made our way through worse.

When they leave she pulls a chair up beside me and strokes my forearm. I am too muddled to maintain much of a conversation.

"Just close your eyes and sleep."

Physicians roll through with running updates on my condition. I have fractures to my scapula, sternum and a thoracic vertebrae. I also have four or five broken ribs. I have some perforations in my right lung, which is only partially collapsed. Hopefully it will inflate with a regimen of breathing exercises. The good news is that my brain scan is unremarkable, which is the way you want it. The shoulder surgeon is uncertain about scapula surgery at this time. There is no obvious bone breakage in my hands. They will be further evaluated by surgeons in Michigan.

"All good news, right?" to which Barbara smiles benignly.

"Yes, John, all good news," a playful shake of her head. "Aren't you a lucky one."

Barbara shares updates in calls to John and Kate. She talks them out of catching flights to Las Vegas.

"We'll be home soon," she assures, without the benefit of a timetable. She begins to sag shortly after hanging up.

"I'm starting to exhale, enough to feel exhausted."

"Climb in," I quip, patting the bed with my good left hand.

Erin wakes us when she rolls in around 6:00 P.M.

"How 'ya doing, Pops?"

She follows with tears and ribbing, and a barrage of nursey questions. We answer what we can. As she becomes more confident that I will recover, she provides a strong dose of perspective.

"There are a lot of shot-up people in here. They've got the young man next door in an induced coma."

Erin sends her mother off to a hotel they have reserved. I'm given medication that releases me to sleep.

But not for long.

Solicitous nurses check and re-check me throughout the night, peppering me with questions I struggle to understand. Erin does her best to interpret and protect. I wake with alarm at any difficulty breathing, the pain that erupts with the slightest movement. Erin assists through all of it, dismissing my concern about her lack of sleep.

CHAPTER 25

THE LIGHTS COME ON SHORTLY after my first extended sleep. Medication dopey, I let Erin navigate through bathing and breakfast, questions and attention from a fresh round of nurses. They wash my hair chemically inside a plastic bag, what feels like the first nod in the direction of normalcy.

"I'm looking good, aren't I?" when Barbara takes over, trying to stifle a smile.

A pulmonologist examines me in the early afternoon. He gives me a schedule of breathing exercises to inflate the deflated area of my lung. I do my best to inhale hard and often, in spite of the spasms that erupt along my broken ribs.

I try to respond with good-natured lucidity to the nonstop visits of specialists throughout the day. Barbara encourages me to relax down into the medicinal haze between consults, rest my broken body needs.

I am feeling stronger by early evening, pestering anyone I can about the lung-healing necessity of getting up and moving. When I wrangle approval from a worn-out resident, Barbara and I get on our way. The hard part is getting out of bed, taking hold of a walker and standing up. Yowser. First steps feel like progress, however stiff and unsteady. Once underway we go as far as I am allowed, earning cautionary attention from members of the staff.

I want out and am willing to walk there.

Barbara and I talk as we travel. She asks what I remember from the crash and I tell her. There are lots of blank spaces. Some specifics begin to surface, the absence of signage or a flagman at the end of the pavement.

"Just fresh asphalt, flying off where it ended. Playground to graveyard, no fence in between." When she says nothing, "I am very lucky."

"It's a good thing you've got some German mettle stirred into that Irish stew of yours. You don't kill easily."

She gives my hand a squeeze and smiles.

We turn around at the end of the corridor and begin the long journey back.

Barbara dozes off after we share what they call dinner. Everyone must be consultation weary, because there is a lull in traffic to my room. I have a few minutes to myself.

This feels like one of those forks in the road — one month shy of seventy-five and broken.

New life or long slide into dotage? Mine to decide.

When Barbara wakes we talk about release and going home. We have a lot of questions about the road ahead. Getting all my physicians in the room at one time is probably a longshot.

We drift back to the accident. Barbara wants details. I tell her about standing over my bike, the key dangling from the ignition, the distance to Encinitas.

She just looks at me, expressionless, and waits. Then she looks down, shakes her head and starts laughing. The eyes that open are full of mischief.

Moored to Barbara and the kids, I will heal up better than before.

I get an uneasy feeling in my chest during shift change on the unit. I ask Barbara to raise my bed a bit.

"You okay?"

"I think so," the best I can do.

"Could you reach me one of those extra pillows?" She does and I pull it against my chest. I cough tentatively to clear my airway, sending myself into a breathless spasm.

"Oh, John, are you okay?"

I am not okay, but struggle to say it, nodding a constricted *no*.

"Get me a nitro, please," I whisper. Barbara grabs her purse, alarm in her eyes.

I place a pill under my tongue and wait. The pain ratchets up. Another pill, but the pain keeps coming, and with it a throbbing in the center of my chest. I squeeze out "Another" as an orderly walks in.

"He's having a heart attack!" Barbara exclaims.

He races out of the room to get help, but doesn't come back. The pain is taking over, way beyond normal angina.

"It's bad," to Barbara who pushes another nitro under my tongue. Then she's out in the hall and shouting,

"He's having a heart attack! He's having a heart attack!"

I'm in a tailspin now, dropping away, dropping.

When I come to, the room is full.

"His heart rate is down to 165."

There's bubbly confusion in my chest, but nowhere near the pressure and pain.

Barbara insists that I be given the heart medication they removed on admitting me to the hospital. They counter with concerns about bleeding. Barbara prevails. Someone rushes off for medication.

The last thing I remember is a discussion about more x-rays.

Erin is with Barbara when I wake up. There are a lot of white coats in a semicircle around the foot of the bed. The supervisor of residents is explaining that they must prepare me for surgery, which yanks me to full attention.

"Surgery? For what?"

She calmly explains that while studying an x-ray they discovered a possible leak in my intestines.

"A shadow in your abdomen," she says, "possibly fluid or air from a perforated bowel."

This can't be happening.

I look over at Barbara in disbelief, but she is focused on the doctor.

"I am not convinced this is a break, but we have to take you back to radiology to check. We have no time to waste. If there is a perforation, we must get you to surgery immediately."

I look back to Barbara. She nods her assent.

"Let's do it," less decision than surrender.

I wake to the chief and a few of her minions.

"As I hoped, we found nothing to indicate a break in your intestines. Everything got pushed around in there when you crashed, creating the shadow that showed up on the portable x-ray."

There's relief on Barbara's face.

"Thank you, Doctor." I catch her at the door when she is leaving.

"Sorry about all the commotion." A flutter of chuckles trails down the hall.

When they are gone, we just look back and forth at each other. Erin is shaking her head. Barbara looks shell-shocked.

"It's time for you to get out of here, Mom. Dad and I can take it from here."

Barbara leans down to kiss me before leaving.

"Please sleep as long as you can," I whisper, the ache of open laughter when I add, "I've got everything under control."

CHAPTER 26

IT IS quiet when I wake, surprising in a hospital that is never quiet. Erin is asleep in the recliner, an open textbook in her lap. She wheezes abruptly, startling herself awake. She jerks to attention, looks over to check me, then drops her head back and rubs her eyes.

"Good morning, Erin."

"Good morning, Dad." She rubs her eyes some more.

"Did you get some sleep?"

"Yes I did," a smile breaking over her face. "After all the drama."

"Drama?"

"Yah, I think you missed the third act. The alarms. The stampede that followed."

"I don't understand."

"Your heart stopped beating when the sinus rhythm was converting back to normal."

"What?"

"You shook us up pretty good."

My head clears somewhat even as the pain worsens. I'm getting to the end of the medication cycle. Barbara and Erin are conferring at the end of my bed, their version of a shift change.

Barbara turns to me with distress when Erin tells her about my heart stopping.

"It was getting boring around here," I shrug with my good left shoulder, trying to make light of it.

Barbara is good at lightness. There is no light in her eyes. I've worn them out. They try to rally, but they are running on empty. Because of me. I crashed and roped them into the clean-up. Not just yesterday and today, but tomorrow and the day after that. A whole string of days after that.

I've been pretty closed in on myself, understandable perhaps, all the pain and such. But it's a lifelong struggle, really. The least I can do is pay better attention to them, lighten the load where I can.

I can start by shedding any notions of victimhood. I brought this on myself. I wanted to take this ride. I benefitted from the miles, the beauty, the solitude. I crashed, no one but me. To whine about anything is absurd — or to wallow in self-loathing for that matter, a particularly pathetic form of self-absorption.

It's time to get my head out of my ass, attend to them and the business of getting better.

Erin is gone when the head of cardiology rolls in. He is young and fit, probably a runner.

"I've read summaries of your history, going way back."

"You must be tired out."

"A little," looking up to smile. "You've been at this for a while."

We go over last night's incidents in detail. He lays out some options we might pursue. He tries not to show relief when Barbara and I promise to pick up the pieces with Rick McNamara, my long-term cardiologist back in Michigan.

"Then you'll release me?"

"I'll sign off. But I'm just a small part of it. You've got a lot of banged-up parts, and specialists for each. Everyone has to sign off before you're cleared for release."

"Today?"

"We'll start rounding them up today."

Good intentions I'm sure, but everyone's busy. The second shift nurse finally admits that release rounds "should begin in the morning."

Barbara and I thank her, then glance at each other when she leaves.

"Montes crescit, noscetur ridiculous mus."

"Stop it, John. What does that mean?"

"The mountains groan, and behold a ridiculous little mouse is born."

"You pleased with yourself?"

Any vestige of humor is long gone by the time Erin takes over. I kiss Barbara and she leaves. My brain also, as the cumulative effect of four days of pain sedation pushes me in the direction of delirium.

The night nurse rouses me out of coma territory to announce that they must "free my bed" by moving me to another unit. This transfer shouldn't hurt as much as it does, given my over-medication. Pain turns to agitation by the time they ease me onto clean sheets in a new bed. In spite of my high-minded resolve, I get pretty crazy. I pepper Erin with delirious insistence that she check on my motorcycle and find the wallet I'm certain has disappeared. I blather uncertainty about the road ahead, much of which doesn't make sense.

"When does this train leave?" is another favorite, obstinate certainty that we are on a train.

Erin attempts to ease my distress during a bumpy night, not once telling me that I am out of my mind. This in spite of regular pronouncements that "I can fly out of here with a red cape, an R on it for *ready*."

CHAPTER 27

BARBARA IS BACK when the first shift nurse cycles in. She expresses concern about the level of my medication. I do not know what gets decided, focusing instead on the nurse's chin-jutted commitment.

"I'm getting you out of here before this shift is done. Period." Then I am back at sea and underwater. Is giving up control different from giving up?

Godot stops by, arguing both sides of the question.

"I can't go on like this."

"That's what you think."

Over and over.

At some point my deceased father stops by. I beg him to rip the top off my life.

I get shaken awake by a series of specialists who ask me questions I pretend to understand. I mostly keep my mouth shut and let Barbara do the talking. One by one they agree to release me, confident of the medical team I have at home.

Barbara rushes off when Erin returns, to fetch clothes large enough to slide over my bandages. I am with the last specialist when she comes back. Whatever reservations he has about my addled brain, he signs me over to Barbara and Erin.

Then I'm sitting in a wheelchair in the cool air outside, waiting for a tardy Uber to arrive. Soon headlights are all around us — *please don't crash* — and a bellman trying to assist by latching onto my busted right side. They are pushing me across a scarlet carpet now, and into the gold confines of an elevator. There is more gold trim in the bathroom of our room as I aim erratically into the swaying toilet bowl. Then bed, the pain of easing down, relief.

"A clean getaway," I mutter before fading away.

CHAPTER 28

THE SUN IS bright when Barbara wakes me, and later when they work me into sweatpants and an oversized hoodie. The sock they slide onto my gouged foot is soft and warm.

Then I am waiting in a wheelchair in a large room at the airport. The pain is cutting me in half. I muscle my way out of the wheelchair in spite of Barbara and Erin's protestations, and move around to ease the pain. We wait for what seems like a long time. I am getting weak and dizzy now, and ask them to help me lie down on the floor. Barbara breaks through my insistence by warning that they may not let me on the plane. I get back in the wheelchair, swallow hard and wait.

They help me to my feet at the end of the ramp onto the plane. Erin smiles our way through the door and steers me down the aisle to a seat facing the wall behind the pilot's cabin. I plead to the stewardess with my eyes when Erin cannot get my seat to lean back. Nothing can be done. The last seat in first class seems to be broken.

"We are on the plane," I whisper to Erin. She buckles me in and retreats, to join her mother in second class.

The passenger to my right is watching me closely. I'm afraid he might blow my cover. I close my eyes as if falling asleep, robbing him of the opportunity to complain. I sit perfectly still until we are in the air, wincing only when turbulence bounces me awake.

I wait for Erin's help before sleepwalking down the empty aisle and off the plane. Barbara is waiting with a wheelchair. I go blank until they help me up into the SUV Kate has wrangled for our three-hour ride back home. I try to hug her, mumble that I am ok. She nods, but there are tears in her eyes.

I am delighted to see Finnegan wagging his tail in the seat behind me. Kate shields me with her forearm from his ninety-pound enthusiasm. He seems to understand, dropping his head on the armrest between us. I rest my good left arm on him, fingers on top of his muzzle.

I give Katie a thumb up and fall asleep before we reach the expressway. I ask to make a restroom stop when I wake up later. She pulls into a Wendy's, and helps me to the restroom, then hands me a chocolate Frosty after she buckles me back in. She slips me a pack of miniature chocolate doughnuts when we make a gas stop later. I munch my way into a warm, dark place from which I will not emerge until morning.

HOME

"We shall not cease from exploration
And the end of our exploring
Will be to arrive where we started
And know the place for the first time."

T.S. Eliot

"Only that day dawns
to which we are awake.
There is more day to dawn."

Henry David Thoreau

CHAPTER 29

MY LEFT EYE is too sticky to open when I blink myself awake. I yelp when I try to raise my right hand to clear it. I recognize the ribbed wood ceiling above me. I am in our bedroom at home.

Barbara's alarm melts into a warm smile when she rushes in and realizes I am okay.

She kneels down beside the bed and leans in, then lowers herself tenderly down over me.

"Don't move. Just lay there. Let me touch you."

When I wake again, the shadows have shifted on the walls of our room. I know better than to move. I am trapped inside my body, like one of those overextended African porters who refuse to journey on until their souls catch up. I will wait inside this body for my brain to catch up. That could take a while.

Barbara follows her smile into the room.

"Good morning, Johnny Boy, afternoon really. How are you?" And when I smile, her hand moves up along my cheek.

"I'm fine, but pretty foggy."

"Foggy is better than pain. I'm just glad you are here, back home."

"Me too."

Barbara helps me up when I insist, and I re-enter the world of pain. I convulse when she helps me swivel, unable to suck in a breath. Rib ends grind against each other when I fight my way to my feet. I spasm when I gasp for air. Barbara holds me as I struggle for balance.

"I have to go."

She assists me as I lurch in the direction of the bathroom, then steadies me as I sway back and forth in front of the toilet. I aim for the bowl, and don't entirely miss.

———

I straggle into the bright openness of the living room, stand long enough to catch my breath.

"How did we get so lucky to live here?"

I shuffle over to the chair that will become home for the immediate future. Barbara winces at my pain when helping me sit down.

Finn bounds up when the girls return from a walk.

He hunches down in front of me when he senses my woundedness. He sniffs the bandages on my hands, knees and ankle, and becomes very quiet.

"It's okay, Buddy," but he seems unconvinced. He will not move away until I do.

I try to smile when Kate asks me how it feels to be home.

The girls get tentative around me, sensing my difficulty with conversation. They comfort and assure, but do not seem assured themselves. Nor do John Ryan and Darcy when they arrive with our granddaughter, Annabelle. John teases me with familiar playfulness, then backs off. The order of the day becomes watch, wait, and help where you can — today, the next day and the next.

I feed on the kids' love and solicitude, but don't have much to give back. I drift in and out of a drug-infused state of disorientation. I ask them how they are doing, then struggle to maintain attention to what they have to say. They are neither used to my withdrawal nor comfortable with it. They try to pretend otherwise. I wake to muffled conversations about Barbara's exhaustion or the extent to which I will recover. I take whispered versions of "will he come back?" into the medicinal cage in which I am confined. My efforts to reassure them seem to fall flat. I can hardly stand the pain of movement, but hate the befuddlement that comes with the medication. I am desperate to get my brain back, or whatever is left of it. Being unable to communicate with these kids is crazy-making, and I am feeling crazy enough.

I'm almost glad their jobs demand that they go back to work. I am moored to their wellbeing, but the day-to-day work of recovery seems less daunting than trying to tamp down their fears.

CHAPTER 30

I CAN DO nothing without Barbara. We shower together so she can wash me down. After helping me dry off, she removes the bandages on my hands, knees, and ankle, changes the dressings as Erin has shown her, then bandages me back up. She cooks our meals and cleans up after my left-handed attempts to feed myself. She oversees the medications I am scheduled to take all hours of the day and night. Most difficult of all, she tempers the impatience I feel about being unable to care for myself.

We are living a latter-day version of routines we developed during a stretch of heart attacks and surgery twenty years ago. You'd think I'd be better at it, but I am not. I rhapsodize about the value of stillness, but I like doing things — pain or no pain. I'm already getting edgy about what I can't do. Moving furniture is one thing, but how about thinking straight? I can't read, write, or carry on a sustained conversation. I'm not okay with that.

It's time to start weaning myself off the pain meds and muscle relaxants. I can handle pain if it comes with clarity.

The weather is warm enough that Finn and I can move outdoors. Even on a difficult day, that feels like relief. Barbara and I live in a small house on a big hill between two lakes. White Lake sprawls from the foot of our dune to the nearest town, seven miles to the east. Finnegan and I spend hours on the deck that overlooks it during uncommonly balmy October days.

When the sun shifts in late afternoon, I hobble through the living room to the front deck that looks out over Lake Michigan to the west. A three-hundred-mile-long glacial gash, she is all horizon, the nearest shore seventy miles away. It's a view like we had from *Grace* mid-Atlantic, calling up memories that distract me from pain.

The summer people have gone back to the city, the arid Southwest, or the moist warmth of the South. This is the season made for writing, but I scribble nonsense when I put pen to paper. What I'm left with is the sun on my face and Finn's soft ear under the fingers of my bandaged hand. And Barbara, only a room away napping back from exhaustion.

Even with an overgrown capacity for self-doubt, I have no gnawing reservations about the trip itself. A softer landing would have been nice, especially for Barbara and the kids. I deeply regret the distress I caused them, the wear and tear on Barbara. But I have no argument with the curiosity and love of extension that spawned it.

I did not cycle away out of boredom or unhappiness with my life. I am crazy about Barbara all these decades later, her brains, her heart, her parts, the life we have built with our children and friends. That she continues to like me is hard to fathom, a longstanding lapse in her considerable lucidity.

I have nothing to acquire or escape.

I would like to inhabit myself more comfortably, and by that path transcend myself. I can start with the adventure right in front of me now, rebalancing a life overreliant on doing, finding the *enough* in this sun-drenched afternoon.

"Do you remember the man who died right behind us in the security line at the airport in Paris?"

"Yes I do, John, as much as I'd like to forget. What makes you think of that?"

"Just how suddenly it happened — talking one moment, then falling over, his head like a bowling ball on the marble floor."

"It was terrible."

"Yes it was, blood leaking out of his broken skull."

"Really, John?"

"He could have been dead before he hit the floor."

"Not over dinner, please." When I say nothing, "but where did that come from?"

"Just thinking how hard my helmet hit the pavement, blood thinners and all, what a gift it is to be sitting here tonight."

We are quiet for a while, just eat, or try to. I drop a piece of potato off the fork I am not mastering with my left hand.

We look at each other and grin.

"You know, I'm not that afraid of death."

"Stop it, John."

"I like living a lot. I don't want to miss any of it, most of all you and the kids. It breaks my heart to think of leaving you."

"Then don't." She puts her fork down and reaches across the table.

It's been an hour since Barbara brought my bedtime medication. I am holding her with my working left arm. She is asleep, her breath soft against me.

Maybe it's time to carve longevity away from living, just focus on how best to live. Right now, in this bed and helpless, unable to do anything but love.

CHAPTER 31

I WAKE in the morning to a wren chirping outside the window. When he takes a break, I can hear Barbara humming in the kitchen. I don't want the pain that comes with movement. I roll my head to the right to see the beachgrass swaying out beyond our bedroom. It is warm enough that Barbara has opened the sliding door. Morning air rides in on the hint of a breeze.

If I were dying, Barbara is the door through which I would pass.

Today the job is to live.

I call Barbara and she comes in smiling with the day's first dose of medication.

"Just half a dose," she assures me.

I put off getting out of bed as long as possible, as if I can avoid the pain. I can't.

We choose to get my shower out of the way after some coffee and eggs. We laugh as she takes a bar of soap to my privates — "oh that's still working" — and a very tender toweling off. I catch a glimpse of my reflection in the mirror above the sink and turn sideways for a better view.

A dark purple cloud, blotchy around the edges, stretches from above my right shoulder across both my chest and back, and down to my bandage-shrouded knee. My shoulder is cantered both forward and down. Both shoulder and arm are swollen to football proportions, all the way down to my furrowed hand.

My face is gaunt and unshaven, bone structure as available as it was in my teens. My eyes are dark and empty, diminished. The musculature on the rest of my frame is diminished also, the easy angularity that seemed like a birthright. Like my father's body when the Parkinson's took over, but without my father's admirable lack of self-consciousness.

"I really did it," I tell Barbara, who is standing behind me.

"Yes, you did." She seems embarrassed for me, adding "you'll bounce back" with less conviction than I'd like.

"That's a lot of bouncing."

Silence does not create feeling. It opens a space into which feelings can emerge, and fester if we let them.

There's too much silence on the deck this morning.

Finn's not talking, nor the ever-present wrens. And there's a lot I'd rather not think about or feel, starting with what I've done to myself.

There's a special word for it in German, something like *torn-to-pieces-hood*. That's the way I'm feeling — not just aged and faded but torn to pieces. If I'm looking for a ticket to decline, I've got it. I wrestle with discouragement into the afternoon, wallow might be a more accurate word. I have growing concerns about what banging my head did to my lagging brain. I think of myself as a writer, but is that still true?

It is dusk before I work my way through sad and scared to challenge.

Accidents happen, accidents and injuries. And I am busted up pretty good.

Can I find the adventure in the wreckage?

Anybody can drive a damn motorcycle across the country.

It's clear I've hit a nerve when I ask Barbara about today's contacts over dinner.

"A lot of people want to talk with you, John. And they're getting jumpy."

I say nothing.

"I've been telling everyone be patient, he's mending, and they're trying to be respectful. But they're pretty worked up. Just how bad is he, and when can we see him?"

"I'm sorry to put you on the spot..."

"That's not the point. I don't know how much longer I can hold the line before people just start showing up."

"Tell them I'll be off the meds in a couple days, that I'm resuming my daily walks."

"Walks?" She's incredulous now.

"How about we start in the morning?"

CHAPTER 32

FINN LEADS the way across the deck, stopping every few steps to look back. Barbara has her hand under my left elbow, my damaged right arm in a sling.

"Slowly, Honey," then "one at a time" when we get to the steps.

I am surprised by how feeble I am, but happy to be underway. We take baby steps down the ski-sloped driveway to the road.

"You doing okay?" every few steps.

"Terrific."

"Isn't this far enough?"

"Just a little farther."

We don't walk that far, but enough that I'm exhausted by the time we get back.

"You did great."

"Further tomorrow," and we both light up.

Barbara goes in to pull dinner together.

"What do you think, Finn?"

All the way down to the mailbox and back? You're killing it.

Grounded is not the same as marooned.

Doing nothing is more difficult than walking.

Barbara brings a copy of *Sailing Grace* out to me on the deck. She opens it to where I've begun a section with a quote from Marcel Proust.

"The real voyage of discovery consists not in seeking new landscapes, but in having new eyes."

"I can't wait to see that clearly."

"Soon, John. You'll be off pain meds entirely in the morning."

The journey from riding to crashing to being still has been abrupt. It's an opportunity, I'm sure, if I can take it. Can I ride through this medicinal haze to awake?

Nurse, gatekeeper and general manager, Barbara is setting up appointments with a series of physicians. She's also keeping track of everything from insurance coverage to the status of my cycle out in California. I catch the end of a conversation when I come into the kitchen for an afternoon snack.

"The motorcycle people," she looks up from her

notes. "The woman said most people driving a motor-cycle this damaged don't live to talk about it."

I try to focus on my good fortune, not the sadness "this damaged" calls up.

Barbara clicks on our favorite news program in the evening. I don't have to think clearly to watch TV, but am not sure how much actually registers. Nothing I say suggests clear headedness. Although she cares too much to say it, Barbara might as well be watching alone.

What seems obvious even in my diminished state is that tonight's offerings are pretty thin soup, stimulation that monopolizes attention without doing much to deepen understanding.

Information is not the enemy any more than thinking is the enemy of awareness. The problem is my almost addictive consumption. Can I turn down the fire-hose a bit, establish more balance between volume and depth?

Barbara has dozed off in the chair beside me. I click off the TV and rouse her.

Lying down in bed yanks me back into my body, spasms from rib to neck. Barbara reaches over and takes my hand. She rolls over to me as I simmer down, and comforts me with her body.

CHAPTER 33

IN MY DREAMS I am at sea again, storm aroused, that overhanging wave, all shoulders and elbows when it breaks, magnifying even the smallest mistake. I wake up shaken and in pain, relieved to be in this bed, this morning.

Barbara stirs at first light. We ease into morning over coffee and tea. I'm taking no pain medication today, which feels like progress. Finn gobbles his breakfast and flops down on the floor between us. I am feeling the burn in every seam, but thinking more clearly in spite of the pain.

"More like myself," I tell her. "Ready to begin taking some calls."

We run through the appointments she has made for me, cardiologist and physical therapist at the top the list.

"Let's see what I can do for myself before talking to the surgeons."

She seems to agree, but not without adding "We do have to check on that scapula and those ribs. Your lung too, and the tendons in your hands."

It's talk that does little for appetite or mood. We drop it and move on.

She tells me the kids will be returning for the weekend.

"They're pretty shook up, John."

"I know. I feel badly about how unavailable I've been. I can do better now that I'm getting off the meds. I hope we can get them laughing again."

"Laughter would be good."

I take a couple of books out on the deck, to see what I can handle. I have trouble focusing for long. Whitman seems to understand:

"Apart from the pulling and hauling stands who I am,

... both in and out of the game."

I am certainly out of the game. His suggestion that there "will never be any more perfection than there is now" leaves me reaching.

Have I so attached my life to *doing*, that simply *being* leaves me empty? What about those roadside moments in New Mexico, with the horses in Utah's canyon?

What's lacking in this moment, the soft breeze in the

high branches? What disappoints in the green/gold transparency of leaves, the handful of sunlight in this upturned palm?

Can I let myself just *be* for a while, attention without escape into action? What remains when I drop the reacting or resisting, altering or fixing, blessing, rejecting, even thinking about, understanding?

Awareness only, without all the extras.

Can I let myself be that?

———

Barbara helps me into my sling for our midday walk. Finn is less solicitous when we get underway, straying out into the beachgrass to sniff around before turning back to check. Barbara asks less regularly if I am okay. I am learning how to move in ways that don't aggravate my pain. We reach the bottom of the driveway and turn onto the road.

"How you doing, Tarzan?"

"Terrific. Let's stretch it out today."

She doesn't mention "too far" or "too much," only smiles when I catch her checking.

We're down in the valley now, past the mailbox and coming to the base of a hill.

"Let's go up."

"You sure?"

"Yup. I've been thinking about that surgeon, how he

said that if I worked real hard I might get back seventy-five percent of what I've lost. Remember that?"

"What I remember is the look on your face. I was hoping you'd go easy on him."

"Seventy-five percent seems a little lame."

What I don't bring up are my fears about my brain. Will I be able to write again?

CHAPTER 34

THE KIDS SEEM to relax a few exchanges into dinnertime banter.

John's "nice to have you back, fog man," signals a welcome tilt in the direction of irreverence.

Kate pulls out her chair to watch the dogs scrounge for food spilling down the front of me.

"The boys have struck it rich."

I dampen the levity when I try to get serious.

"All kidding aside, I am sorry to put you through this. I know it's been difficult, like my heart was when you were kids."

"It's okay, Dad..." from Erin, always empathetic.

"Thanks, but it's not okay. It's been scary and it's been hard, and that's on me. I took the ride and I crashed. And your mom and you are having to deal with it. I am sorry for that."

"Enough, Dad. We get it." John's not good with apology.

"I'm going to be okay. Better in fact. But I don't have much control over how feeble I am right now, how depressed I feel, how quiet..."

"A little more quiet, please," John again.

"Alright, I get it. Just know I'm gonna make something good out of this."

"We get it, Dad." There's no stopping Kate when she gets exasperated. "Attitude, gratitude, find the frickin pony in the shit. We know, we know." Nods and eye rolling around the table, Annabelle's hand up over her mouth.

"Even me, Papa John," palms up now. "We all know."

"I guess I've mentioned this before," to Barbara, at the other end of the table.

"You think?" And we are laughing so hard Darcy grabs a pillow to cushion my ribs.

I laugh myself awake during the night — "we know, we all know, Papa John."

"You okay?" Barbara stirs, then dozes off when I assure her.

And they're okay, these kids of ours, enough that I can lighten up a bit. I have taught them what I can about living. I cannot protect them from what life brings, or fix what only they can fix. They are smart and strong and independent. They will figure out what must be figured, without their father's platitudes.

I can accompany them where they let me, attention without all the answers.

CHAPTER 35

BARBARA and I begin our tour of physical therapists and physicians. My therapist introduces me to a set of tortures she calls stretching exercises, without which I may never regain my range of motion.

The scapula will probably not need surgery, nor the ribs, only one of which is not well aligned. The status of my lung is still uncertain, but should heal with time and breathing exercises. The vertebrae and sternum will heal on their own. My hands also, although surgery may be needed later to remove debris.

Barbara exhales and grins when she settles into the driver's seat after my last appointment.

"Do you have any idea how lucky you are?"

I am dictating emails now, keeping them short because Barbara is doing the typing until my hands heal. I am also seeing a few friends and relatives for visits Barbara tries to limit to an hour.

"You know what a blabbermouth he can be. He needs his energy to heal."

Mostly I'm doling out iPhone assurance, from a playful "there's nothing wrong with high flying, so long as you can handle the ground" to the more sober "I've lost a little in the old noggin, but I've got what I've got." I remind a politically distressed friend how knowing someone takes the wind out of judging, to another how perceptions tend to be both accurate and incomplete.

"Including yours and mine" doesn't go down well.

I suggest to a client that she treat herself as well as she would treat me, and to a litigious other that I'm not planning to sue anyone.

"I don't remember all the particulars, but neither do I feel like a victim."

I talk with a longtime friend who can't imagine me "sitting around, doing nothing."

"That makes two of us. Probably a good thing to work on."

When he persists, I remind him how the composer Stravinsky, after a devastating stroke, responded to friends concerned at his relegation to a wheelchair on his Paris balcony. When they asked him what he did all day, he responded "J' attende."

"It translates freely to 'I watch' or 'I pay attention'."

"That works for you?"

"I wouldn't go that far, but I'm trying."

After we hang up I get to thinking about an afternoon at an art museum in Amsterdam, the crush of people following their cameras around. They were clicking away as if underwater with periscopes. How surreal it seemed, what Coetzee called "the difference between living in the real world and living in a world of representations."

I've certainly done my time in the world of representations. I need more time with Stravinsky.

CHAPTER 36

I TALK Barbara into longer walks in the woods near our home. I pay close attention to every step, as missteps buy me a whole lot of hurt. The pain is becoming more manageable week to week, even without the meds. It takes more to trigger it, but when I do, it still packs a wallop. Eyes on the trail, John, like driving a motorcycle.

Walking alone feels like a big step forward. Walking without an arm sling feels like another. Surgery on my scapula is finally off the table, but I am unable to raise my arm above my chest. It's all about breaking through scar tissue now, regaining strength and range of motion.

"I'll be able to throw a football soon," on my last visit to the shoulder surgeon. He raises his eyebrows, smiles, but says nothing.

"Thirty yards by summer."

I groan out loud trying to lift the phone when Larry calls from California.

"It's nice hearing from you too, John," he bellows, the familiar derision of a sixty-year friend.

We move quickly past my tale of woe to a mystery ailment he's been struggling with since summer.

"Low sodium levels, they keep telling me. Nobody can figure out why. I have no energy, can't do a thing."

"I'm sorry, Larry. I wish I didn't know that territory."

We commiserate playfully, then get serious.

"So how do you deal with it, John?"

"Best I can, which isn't saying much. I feel pretty useless a lot of the time, can't write a lick. Last week I tacked a new job description above my desk."

"Yeah..."

"Number one: 'Love everyone, including your miserable self.'

"Number two: 'Everything else'."

"Hmm..."

"Just to remind myself."

I get a muddled call from Larry when I'm out on a walk a few days later. His voice is raspy, almost unintelligible.

"It's cancer, John. Metastasized from my brain to my liver."

"Jeez, Larry, I'm so sorry."

The numbers are devastating, a matter of time.

He can't talk for long.

"They've got me on something that's screwing up my brain. Wish me some of that Otterbacher luck."

Barbara is humming over a new recipe when I get back to the house. I break down telling her about Larry. She is distressed about Larry and Anne as well, the harsh road down, so little we can do.

A Judy Collins song comes on the radio in the background, "Who knows where the time goes?"

Barbara looks over at me and nods. "Good question."

"Wherever it's going, it's going fast."

"It's hard sometimes not to feel like you're losing ground."

"We are losing Larry," I answer too abruptly, "and we can't do anything about it."

"Be grateful for the time we've had, I guess."

She's right, but I'm not there yet. I don't say anything for a few tense moments, searching for a way to pivot.

"I sure as hell don't want to waste what I've got." Face to face now. "You. This moment."

She smiles. We kiss.

"You do have me," back to cutting vegetables, "...the first time you opened your mouth."

I wander into the living room after doing dishes, stoop down to where Finn leans into my hand.

"You don't spend time worrying about this stuff, do you?"

He leans in further.

I move over to the fireplace and turn around to warm my backside. The firelight dances on the wall across from me.

It's all change when I am paying attention, transience baked into the cake. Nothing I can do to stop it. Can I weld distress into a deepened appreciation for every fleeting moment?

Death will call the question.

CHAPTER 37

WE ARE SEEING a lot of Kate and her boyfriend, Nate. They've purchased *Grace* from us and are preparing for a sabbatical cruise, taking fantasy to plan with a lot of hard work. They spend most weekends getting their hands dirty, fiberglass and engine oil, hairline cuts from a mile of re-wiring.

Kate stays behind to talk after breakfast. I welcome the opportunity because she is the most verbally reserved of our kids.

The dam breaks early. She reminds me that she has kept "pretty buttoned up" about my motorcycling. Then she breaks down while talking about the anguish she feels.

"I want you to do what you want. But know that I am terrified at the idea of you cycling off again. Terrified at what could happen to you and to us." She is weeping now.

"The idea of you dead or paralyzed or brain damaged haunts me, Dad. I love you and need you and I can't bear the thought of losing you."

Both of us are crying now.

"I know you love the adventure of cycling, and don't want to stop. And it's your decision. But you are not in this alone. What you decide affects me."

She stands up when I approach her and gather her up in my good left arm. We hang onto each other.

"I wish we had talked about this earlier, Katie. I'm proud of you for telling me now. Thank you for being so honest. I love you."

"I love you too, Dad."

Barbara and I have a long talk after Kate leaves. I do too much of the talking, venting mostly, grief and guilt, loss, the bankruptcy of victimhood.

"There's adventure beyond motorcycling," I tell her, clearly talking to myself. "If I can't find it, shame on me."

Barbara smiles and nods.

"This is a tough one, John. Take your time with it."

She puts her arms around me.

"I support you, whatever you decide."

I take Finn for a walk when Barbara leaves for the grocery store. An hour into the woods, we plop down on a sandy ledge next to the lake. Finn sits facing me, all grins now. His eyes are full of light. Past and future mean nothing to him. He lives comfortably in the present, except perhaps for the hunger that growls in him with the approach of dawn and dusk.

I want some of that wisdom now. I know how *have to* can suck the energy out of *choose to*, reducing opportunity to obligation, or worse yet, a burden. That's no way to live.

I am not a victim. This is a choice, not a sentence. However much I love motorcycling, I live for what I have with Barbara and the kids. Simple as that. The last thing I want is to cause them pain.

It will take some time to let go of cycling. I will never let go of what I have with my Honda, how we've traveled and where, the awe and ache and satisfaction at the end of the day. Can I cherish memory without shackling myself to it, letting the past cloud what I have today?

Is the story of my life *what's lost* or *what remains?*

CHAPTER 38

THE DAYS ARE FLYING BY, the weeks, and with
them some of the pain. I stretch my way through frozen
scar tissue in my shoulder, back and hands. Long walks
are a staple of the day. On the way to the lighthouse in a
stiffening breeze, turkey vultures circle, trolling for prey.
They call up the darkened cliffs in Utah, feeding bats
and free-wheeling hawks. How perfect it seemed, a
church with no roof.

I call Larry as I walk. Anne picks up. Larry is asleep.
Anne talks in understatement about his condition, but
her tone and tentativeness are clear. I do not ask about
timelines. I tell her I will come. She is noncommittal,
uncertain whether it will help or be more painful. We
leave it there.

Will nothing stand still?

I am devastated about Larry and his family, the loss
of a life-long friend. We have known each other since

we were kids, and I'm not going to make any new old friends. I get to choose how I respond, but that's all. It has a lot in common with my accident that way. I can whine or resist, play the hapless victim, or work my way to some wry acceptance.

It's simple, really, *let go or be dragged.*

Barbara gives me the five-minute dinner warning when I get back to the house. We talk about Larry and Anne for a while, then settle down at the dinner table.

Larry's dying and my near brush with death has ramped up the importance of our time together, the attention I pay to Barbara or fail to. We will not be given this dinner again, every moment a one-take, every hour.

This is it. Age does not forgive inattention.

Shadows are taking over at dusk. I open the slider and step outside. November is on a rampage, green going yellow in the billowing seagrass, scarlet in the rioting leaves. Everything is alive in its own way and dies.

Less and less a stranger here, I talk to the sunrise like I did at sea, the sunset also. They do not answer, only invite me into the larger life we share.

I step inside to get a jacket, then back into the wind. Geese honk by in the purple overhead, ride accelerating northerlies to the south. Fortress clouds are rolling in, temperature dropping fast. I pull the jacket around me.

With all due respect to the soft invitation of dawn, the feverish intensity of noon, is there anything more beautiful than sunset and the enveloping night?

The throbbing wind wakes me during the night, a spasm in my shoulder. I gradually relax back into what I have, Barbara beside me, the kids at a distance, the dog snoring in the corner of our room.

The future is uncertain, writing and the rest. Doesn't that make it just another adventure? I don't have to understand to embrace it. It is all very rich — stream or flood makes no matter. Can I just let it wash around me, sweep me out into the open, the disappearing edge between everything and me?

CHAPTER 39

BARBARA JOINS me on the deck in the morning, armed with a steaming cup of tea. She is calm, rested and typically upbeat. Finn straggles out behind her, nose in the air to sample overnight offerings. He reaches up to paw sticky sleep from his eye. He shakes himself awake so hard he almost stumbles over. He looks back at us, breakfast on his mind.

Barbara snugs her robe up around her and smiles contentment. We discuss our plans for the day. She finishes her tea and goes inside to feed Finn and take a shower.

I kiss Barbara before she leaves for the city, then pull on my boots and take Finn to the woods. I need some exercise to clear my head and take a fresh-eyed reckoning.

My life is a gift, pure and simple, in-spite of large

parts I don't control. I have a damaged heart and some broken parts, the attrition of age on body and brain. There's not a lot I can do about that, or Larry for that matter.

I have some fears about the road ahead, especially my ability to write. If I can't remember the titles of movies and books, the names of even my favorite authors, is it realistic to think I can corral ideas and experience with words?

How will I know without trying?

Our afternoon walk turns into a marathon. By the time Finnegan and I return from the woods I am drenched with sweat, both effort and resolve. I am seventy-four, but with more than a touch of eleven-year-old. Neither of us believes that writing is behind me.

I stop in the kitchen, cold water for the pooch and a glass for me. I splash water in my face then head for the bathroom, grab a towel and give myself a hearty work-over. When I glance up, there is no hesitation on the face in the mirror.

The road forward begins right here.

Finnegan follows me to my desk and looks up for permission. When I settle into my chair he works his way under the desk, arranging himself on my feet.

A gust of wind launches leaves against the window

above my desk. I close my laptop and switch off the phone, exile the dictatorial "things to do" list to a drawer in my desk. I take out a pad of paper and place it in front of me. I feel a wave of insecurity I choose to call excitement.

I pick up a pen with my bandaged right hand.

"Yes—the springtimes needed you.
Often a star was waiting for you to notice it.
A wave rolled toward you out of the distant past,
or as you walked under an open window,
a violin yielded itself to your hearing.
All this was mission. But could you accomplish it?"

Rainer Marie Rilke
(translated by Stephen Mitchell)

"You will find yourself finally
wanting to forget all enclosures,
including the enclosure of yourself."

Mary Oliver

EPILOGUE

IT STORMED last night with such a fury there were tiny waves in the toilet bowl. It blew through, of course, as storms always do. You stay at the helm until they pass. Although I cannot relive the storms I've been in, I am grateful they travel with me

It has been three years since that last great storm. What began as a journey ended abruptly in a field of rocks, a hard-edged and necessary stillness.

I did not ride out to escape anything, or to get to any particular destination. My intent was to take a break from what I call normal and to explore the natural beauty of people and places off the beaten path. To explore also the erosion of age and what's left of me when I set aside the thinking and doing and interacting with familiar others with which I prop up my frail sense of self.

What remains is what is always available, with a

little more clarity and a little less pretense. Life beyond the hunger of youth, résumé, accumulation, any recitation of events. The love I have for Barbara and our children, friends near and far and still unmet. A tenacious affection for people as they are, both the beauty and the pain. A deepened appreciation for awareness itself, one and done every moment, registered or not.

I do not believe my life is behind me, all adventure in the rear-view mirror. If anything, an energizing tension grows between my curiosity and biology, yielding a being at once seventy-eight and eleven.

Both of us were on board when my Honda took to the air, flying, flying, until very suddenly we were not.

Both travel within my reclaimed body, the stillness-honed shock of raw awareness, knowing rather than knowing about.

I am old, but don't much feel that way, more a willful child with some aches and pains. Truth is, I have never felt more alive, some weird hybrid of challenge and contentment. I am no stranger to distraction or distress, regret for any pain I've caused, the past and what to do with it. Nor has time tempered my gnawing agitation with injustice and inequity in an overheating world. Age is not a place to hide from what needs changing. I am old, but I still have a voice, can carry a sign, and use a pen to raise awareness. Retreat is out of the question.

I discovered early I was more interested in God than doctrine, only later that I could not think my way to what exists beyond thought. The binary brain is good at parts, but hapless in the face of Only. What I can do is relish the questions themselves and pay attention to people and things that might otherwise go unnoticed. Not the mission I expected, but mission nonetheless.

I am fueled in all this by what I have with Barbara, episodes also of slacked-jawed amazement. The wind and beachgrass at play outside the window, calling me out of my contracted self, inviting full immersion.

What I sense these days is that larger dance, a unity within everything I call separate — breeze and trees, desert, sea, my heart and every other. A beauty that defies thickened reading glasses and time, smiles at the notion of distance.

Being itself.

Nothing I can measure or prove, much less capture in words. If I were smarter I wouldn't try.

Even as I write this, I know I will try again. To a crazy old man with hair afire, the lure of an icewater pond. A life on fire, the joy of extension, the possibility of giving off some warmth and some light. But not on this day, this page, Finnegan's nudged insistence under my elbow, a promised walk in the woods before dark.

If the unexamined life, as Socrates suggests, is less worth living, perhaps the same can be said of the over-examined life. Balance matters. It's well past time to unshackle my brain and let the dogs run free.

Banging down a rutted two track yanks me back into my body. Finn prances eagerly in the seat behind me, eyes alight and tongue adangle. He bounds out of the car when I open the door, and darts in the direction of a familiar trailhead. He looks back to make sure I am still with him.

This is it, Boss.

Aren't we lucky?

We enter a stand of depression-era trees and walk down an aisle thinned out in the contest for sunlight. The wrecked remains of the fallen lean against their stronger neighbors, or dissolve into the needle-strewn ground. Without light, death — all of us.

The earth is soft beneath my boots, the kind of terrain that coaxed me off the blacktop, to roll out a sleeping bag before dark. Those days will ride with me as long as there is light. Like being itself, we cannot be apart.

A chipmunk scampers as Finn ambles by. A scruffy blackbird on a bare branch calls me to attention, the breath in the high branches and the tan dog galloping, the earnest woodpecker, black and gray, pausing his work on a weary white pine.

Awareness is the gift, precious and brief.

This moment, empty and abundant, everything I think I am falling away. Only trees and trail now, dog and dwindling light.

ACKNOWLEDGMENTS

All my life I have been standing on the shoulders of generous others, appearing taller than I am. *What Remains* is no exception. Many of you have encouraged, assisted, and put up with me along the way. To call out each of you would fill pages.

I would like to acknowledge Angela Morse, Ed Gaydos, Hank Meijer, Tim Coder, Bette VanDinther, Glen Peterson, Sandra VanderZicht, Dick Holm, Karen Shear, Cathy Weisbeck, Bob VanderMolen, Reinder Van Til and Buck Matthews for your crucial editorial assistance. Dan Hendrickson, Colleen Tallen and Pierre Camy also, and bookcover maven, Willem Mineur.

None of this would matter without Barbara and our family, both wind and harbor for my small life. Our friends also, and my parents before them, who gave much and travel with me everywhere I go.

What Remains belongs to each of you.

ABOUT THE AUTHOR

Psychologist, former state representative and senator, long-distance sailor and motorcyclist, John Otterbacher has written for professional and travel publications in the United States and Europe.

His first book, *Sailing Grace*, was honored as "Best New Non-fiction Book of the Year" by National Indie Excellence Awards and Finalist for Best Books Awards by USA Book News.

He and Barbara live in Michigan, where he is working on a new book.

www.johnotterbacher.com

9 781737 699514